Table of Contents

~ONE: Making Exercise Effortless~ 3

~TWO: Building Micro-Habits~ 17

~THREE: Excellence Through Simplicity~ 28

~FOUR: Recovery as Performance~ 41

~FIVE: The Forge of Champions~ 53

~SIX: Movement as Medicine~ 64

~SEVEN: Where Excellence Begins~ 76

~EIGHT: The Sacrifice Filter~ 89

~NINE: The Leadership Evolution~ 101

~TEN: The Art of Human Connection~ 113

~ELEVEN: Emotional Regulation Under Pressure~ 125

~TWELVE: Breaking Mental Loops~ 138

~THIRTEEN: The FIRE Movement~ 152

~FOURTEEN: Overcoming Scarcity~ 164

~FIFTEEN: Systematic Wealth Building~ 178

~SIXTEEN: Generosity and Safety Nets~ 191

~SEVENTEEN: Finding Flow States~ 206

~EIGHTEEN: Systems Over Goals~ 219

~NINETEEN: Deep Focus in a Distracted World~ 230

~TWENTY: Adaptive Productivity~ 242

~TWENTY-ONE: Creating Meaningful Rituals~ 255

~TWENTY-TWO: Values-Driven Transformation~ 267

~TWENTY-THREE: Finding Meaning Through Adversity~ 281

Copyright Disclaimer

© 2025 by John Shoufler. All rights reserved.

No part of this publication may be reproduced, distributed, or transmitted in any form or by any means, including photocopying, recording, or other electronic or mechanical methods, without the prior written permission of the publisher, except in the case of brief quotations embodied in critical reviews and certain other non-commercial uses permitted by copyright law.

For permission requests, please contact John Shoufler at johnshoufler@booksandguidespro.com.

The information in this book is intended to be a general resource for career development and job search strategies. The author and publisher disclaim any liability in connection with the use of this information. This book is not intended as legal, financial, or professional advice, and individuals should consult with appropriate professionals for guidance in their specific circumstances.

All company names, products, logos, and trademarks mentioned in this book are the property of their respective owners and are used for identification purposes only. Use of these names, logos, or trademarks does not imply endorsement.

~ONE: Making Exercise Effortless~

I used to believe that exercise was supposed to hurt. That if I wasn't gasping for air, drenched in sweat, or pushing through pain, I wasn't doing it right. This mentality kept me trapped in cycles of intense workouts followed by weeks of avoidance. I would start strong, burn out quickly, and then feel guilty about not maintaining the punishing routine I had convinced myself was necessary.

This destructive pattern continued for years. I'd join gyms with enthusiasm, hire trainers who promised to "whip me into shape," and download apps that celebrated burning muscles and exhaustion as badges of honor. Each new attempt followed the same trajectory: initial motivation, increasing intensity, inevitable burnout, and then shame-filled abandonment. I genuinely believed this was just how fitness worked—that some people had the willpower to push through the suffering, and I simply wasn't one of them.

My perspective shifted completely when I discovered the story of Victoria Garrick, a Division I volleyball player at the University of Southern California. Her journey, documented in research conducted by California State University, Fullerton and featured in CSUF News (2019), revealed a truth that would transform how I understood the relationship between movement and mental health.

Victoria stood six feet tall on the volleyball court, her athletic frame commanding attention as she prepared to serve. To outside observers, she embodied collegiate athletic success. She had earned a scholarship to one of the nation's top volleyball programs, competed at the highest level of college athletics, and seemed to have achieved every young athlete's dream. But beneath the surface, she was drowning in anxiety, depression, and perfectionism that would eventually force her to confront everything she thought she knew about strength.

"I was exercising as a form of self-punishment," Garrick revealed in interviews published by CSUF News following her mental health advocacy work. "Every workout was about earning my worth, proving I deserved to take up space, compensating for what I saw as my failures."

This punitive relationship with movement created a vicious cycle that many athletes never escape. The more pressure she put on herself to be perfect, the more exercise became associated with stress, judgment, and shame. Her Instagram feed showed smiling photos in USC gear, but her private reality involved panic attacks before practice, obsessive calorie counting, and a constant fear that she wasn't good enough. Instead of movement being a source of strength and joy, it became another arena where she could fail, another opportunity to fall short of impossibly high standards.

During her junior year, despite her athletic achievements, Garrick found herself struggling with severe anxiety and depression that medications and traditional therapy couldn't fully address. The very activities that were supposed to make her feel strong and capable were instead contributing to her mental health crisis. She was caught in what researchers now recognize as a common trap: using exercise as a weapon against herself rather than a tool for healing.

The culture around her reinforced these destructive patterns. In the high-pressure world of Division I athletics, pain was seen as weakness leaving the body. Exhaustion was proof of commitment. Anyone who couldn't maintain the grueling pace was labeled as lacking mental toughness. This toxic environment, combined with social media's constant display of seemingly perfect athletic bodies, created a perfect storm of self-destruction disguised as discipline.

Garrick's recovery journey began when she finally admitted that her approach to exercise was destroying her from the inside out. She took the brave step of speaking openly about her struggles, first with teammates and coaches, then publicly through social media and speaking engagements. This vulnerability, documented in her TED Talk "The Hidden Opponent" (2019), revealed something profound.

She learned that exercise could be medicine instead of punishment. This wasn't just a philosophical shift—it was backed by emerging neuroscience that showed how movement, when approached correctly, literally rewires the brain for resilience. Working with sports psychologists and mental health professionals, Garrick began to deconstruct years of harmful conditioning about what exercise should feel like.

"I had to completely relearn what it meant to move my body," Garrick explained in subsequent interviews. "Instead of asking 'How can I punish myself today?' I started asking 'How can I take care of myself today?' That one question changed everything."

This simple shift in framing created profound changes in her relationship with movement. On days when she felt anxious, instead of punishing herself with brutal workouts, she might choose gentle yoga or a peaceful walk. When she felt strong and energized, she could still challenge herself athletically, but from a place of joy rather than judgment. Exercise became a dialogue with her body rather than a dictatorship over it.

Research emerging from Garrick's experience and similar cases revealed that when we shift our relationship with exercise from punishment to self-care, from perfection to progress, from intensity to consistency, movement becomes one of our most powerful tools for mental health and overall resilience. Her transformation wasn't about finding the perfect workout routine or achieving a certain level of fitness. It was about discovering that exercise could be gentle, nurturing, and healing.

While Victoria Garrick was learning to transform her relationship with exercise on land, another athlete was making similar discoveries in the water. Michael Phelps's story, which I learned about through Bob Bowman's book "The Golden Rules" (2016) and various Sports Illustrated features, provided another crucial piece of the puzzle.

Phelps didn't start swimming to become a champion. His mother, Debbie, enrolled him in swimming at age seven because she was looking for a way to help her hyperactive son channel his boundless energy. Phelps had been diagnosed with ADHD at age six, and traditional approaches to managing his condition weren't working adequately. Teachers complained that he couldn't sit still, couldn't focus on lessons, and was disrupting other students. The family tried various interventions, including medication, but nothing seemed to provide lasting relief.

"Swimming gave me something that nothing else could," Phelps reflected in interviews documented in Sports Illustrated (2016). "It gave me a place where my mind could quiet down, where all that energy could go somewhere productive, where I could find a rhythm that made sense."

What Phelps discovered, without fully understanding the neuroscience at the time, was that consistent, rhythmic movement has a profound impact on brain function, particularly for those with ADHD. The repetitive nature of swimming—stroke after stroke, breath after breath, lap after lap—created a moving meditation that helped regulate his nervous system in ways that sitting still never could. The bilateral movement of swimming, engaging both sides of the body in coordinated action, helped integrate brain function and improve focus.

The structure and routine of training provided something his ADHD brain craved: predictability in an otherwise chaotic internal world. While his thoughts might race uncontrollably in a classroom, in the pool they synchronized with his movements. The physical exhaustion from training didn't deplete him—it actually helped him focus better in school and manage his symptoms throughout the day.

Later in his career, Phelps faced periods of severe depression that threatened to derail his success. During these dark times, documented in his autobiography "Beneath the Surface" (2016), the pool became his sanctuary. After his second DUI arrest in 2014, Phelps contemplated suicide. But returning to the water, not for competition but for healing, became part of his recovery process.

"People think elite training is about pushing yourself to the breaking point every day," Phelps explained in interviews with NBC Sports (2016).

"But for me, it was about creating a routine that made everything else in my life possible. The training wasn't the hard part—it was the part that made the hard parts manageable."

His coach, Bob Bowman, understood this intuitively. Rather than focusing solely on times and technique, Bowman created training environments that supported Phelps's mental health. Regular training became a form of therapy, providing structure, purpose, and neurochemical regulation that no medication could match. The pool became a place where Phelps could process emotions, work through challenges, and find peace in the rhythm of movement.

These stories led me to dive deeper into the science behind movement as medicine. Dr. John Ratey, a Harvard psychiatrist, calls exercise "Miracle-Gro for the brain" in his book "Spark: The Revolutionary New Science of Exercise and the Brain" (2008). His research reveals that physical movement triggers a cascade of beneficial neurochemical changes more powerful than most antidepressant medications.

When we exercise, our brains undergo remarkable transformations. Within minutes of beginning movement, our brains release endorphins—natural opioids that improve mood and reduce pain perception. Norepinephrine floods our system, enhancing focus and attention while helping to build stress resilience. Dopamine, the motivation and reward neurotransmitter, increases, making us feel more capable and optimistic. Perhaps most remarkably, exercise stimulates the production of brain-derived neurotrophic factor (BDNF), a protein that literally grows new brain cells and strengthens neural connections.

A groundbreaking study published in the Journal of Psychiatric Research (2018) found that moderate aerobic exercise was as effective as antidepressant medication for treating mild to moderate depression. The researchers followed 200 adults with depression, randomly assigning them to either exercise, medication, or a combination. After 16 weeks, all groups showed similar improvements, but the exercise group had lower relapse rates at the one-year follow-up.

But here's what changed my entire approach: these benefits don't require extreme intensity or hours of training. Research published in the American Journal of Preventive Medicine (2019) showed that as little as 15 minutes of moderate movement can trigger significant neurochemical changes. The study followed over 400,000 adults for eight years and found that those who exercised just 15 minutes daily had a 14% reduced risk of mortality and a 3-year longer life expectancy compared to inactive individuals.

A twenty-minute walk can activate many of the same benefits as an intense gym session. The key isn't the difficulty of the exercise—it's the consistency of the practice. This understanding completely revolutionized how I thought about movement and its role in mental health.

Further research published in Translational Psychiatry (2021) revealed that the mental health benefits of exercise follow what researchers call a "dose-response curve." While some movement is always better than none, the optimal mental health benefits occur at relatively moderate levels of activity—about 45 minutes, three to five times per week. Exercising more than 90 minutes at a time or more than 23 times per month was actually associated with worse mental health outcomes, suggesting that the "more is better" mentality can backfire.

This understanding completely transformed how I approached movement. Instead of forcing myself through punishing workouts that left me depleted, I began focusing on gentle, consistent movement that left me energized. Instead of measuring success by how much I suffered, I measured it by how I felt afterward. Did I have more energy? Was my mood more stable? Could I focus better on my work? These became my new metrics for successful exercise.

I started implementing what Victoria Garrick had discovered through her recovery: asking myself "How can I take care of myself today?" rather than "How hard can I push myself?" Some days, taking care meant a challenging workout that tested my limits—but only when my body felt ready and eager for that challenge. Other days, it meant a gentle walk around my neighborhood or a restorative yoga session. The shift from punishment to self-care made movement sustainable in a way that intensity-focused approaches never could.

The transformation required letting go of several myths I had internalized about exercise over decades of cultural conditioning. Each myth had seemed like truth, reinforced by fitness magazines, social media influencers, and well-meaning but misguided advice.

I had to release the intensity myth—the belief that I needed to exercise at maximum effort to gain benefits. This myth was so deeply ingrained that I initially felt guilty doing "easy" workouts. Research published in Medicine & Science in Sports & Exercise (2019) showed that moderate, consistent movement actually provides more sustainable mental health benefits than sporadic intense sessions. The study found that people who exercised at moderate intensity for 30 minutes, five times per week, showed greater improvements in depression and anxiety symptoms than those who did high-intensity workouts three times per week.

I also had to abandon the duration myth—the idea that I needed to exercise for at least an hour to make it worthwhile. Studies in the International Journal of Behavioral Nutrition and Physical Activity (2020) demonstrated that even ten-minute movement breaks throughout the day can accumulate to provide significant health benefits. The research showed that three 10-minute walks produced similar improvements in blood pressure and mood as one continuous 30-minute walk.

The perfection myth was perhaps the hardest to release. I had believed I needed perfect form, ideal conditions, and specialized equipment to exercise properly. This myth kept me from moving on days when I couldn't get to the gym or didn't have the "right" clothes. But research consistently shows that any movement is better than no movement, and that perfectionism actually becomes a barrier to consistent practice.

Finally, I had to let go of the competition myth—the notion that exercise was about beating others or constantly improving my previous performance. This myth had turned movement into another source of stress rather than stress relief. Movement could simply be about maintaining physical and mental well-being, without any competitive element whatsoever.

Actionable Steps:

How to implement: Start tomorrow by committing to just 10 minutes of movement that feels good to your body. This could be walking around your block, stretching while watching TV, dancing to three favorite songs, or any activity that doesn't feel like punishment. Keep a simple log on your phone or in a notebook, rating your mood and energy on a 1-10 scale before and after movement. After one week, review your logs to identify which types of movement consistently improve your ratings.

When to do it: Choose a consistent time that naturally fits into your existing routine. If you always have coffee at 7 AM, make your movement happen right after. If you take a lunch break at noon, use the first 10 minutes for movement. The specific time matters less than linking it to an existing habit. Set a phone reminder with a positive message like "Time to take care of yourself" rather than "Workout time." Continue the reminder for 30 days until the habit becomes automatic.

Why this works: Starting with just 10 minutes removes the overwhelming barrier of hour-long workout commitments that lead to procrastination and avoidance. By focusing on movement that feels good rather than hard, you're literally rewiring your brain's association with exercise from stress to pleasure. The daily consistency, regardless of intensity, builds neural pathways that make movement feel natural and necessary, like brushing your teeth. Tracking your emotional state provides immediate, tangible evidence of the mental health benefits, creating a positive feedback loop that sustains the practice long-term. Research from the European Journal of Applied Psychology (2020) shows that people who approach exercise as self-care rather than obligation are five times more likely to maintain consistent practice over multiple years, and report 60% higher life satisfaction scores compared to those who exercise from a punishment mindset.

~TWO: Building Micro-Habits~

I thought I had discovered the secret to lasting change. Exercise could be medicine rather than punishment, and I understood the neurochemical benefits intellectually. Yet I found myself constantly battling inconsistency. Some days I would embrace my walk with enthusiasm. Other days, despite knowing exactly how much better I would feel afterward, I would find excuses, postpone, or skip entirely. The internal resistance felt irrational, but it was powerful enough to derail my progress repeatedly.

The breakthrough came when I discovered two researchers whose work would fundamentally change how I understood behavior change. Charles Duhigg, a New York Times reporter, had uncovered the neurological mechanics of habits while investigating corporate culture transformation. BJ Fogg, a Stanford behavioral scientist, had developed a revolutionary approach to making change sustainable by starting impossibly small. Together, their insights revealed why my brain was sabotaging my best intentions and, more importantly, how to work with my neurology rather than against it.

Charles Duhigg's journey into habit science began with a personal mystery. As he documented in "The Power of Habit" (Random House, 2012), he found himself automatically buying a chocolate chip cookie every afternoon around 3:30. This wasn't a conscious decision—it was completely automatic. His investigation into this seemingly trivial behavior led him deep into neuroscience laboratories at MIT and other institutions, where researchers were uncovering the fundamental mechanics of human behavior.

Through his research, Duhigg discovered the neurological habit loop—a three-part pattern encoded in the basal ganglia that governs much of what we do automatically each day. Every habit follows the same structure: a cue triggers a routine, which delivers a reward. Once established, this loop operates below conscious thought, which explains why I could intend to exercise in the morning but find myself on the couch without remembering the decision to skip my workout.

Duhigg's cookie habit revealed the deeper dynamics at play. The cue was a mid-afternoon energy dip combined with social isolation. The routine was getting up, taking the elevator to the cafeteria, buying a cookie, and chatting with colleagues. But here was the crucial insight: the reward wasn't the sugar rush. It was the brief social interaction and mental break that recharged him for the afternoon's work.

Once he understood this pattern, Duhigg could experiment with different routines that delivered the same reward. He started walking to colleagues' desks for brief conversations or taking short walks around the building. The cue and reward remained constant, but by changing the routine, he eliminated the unwanted cookie consumption while still meeting his actual need for social connection and mental refreshment.

This discovery illuminated why my attempts at consistent exercise felt like such a battle. I was trying to override deeply embedded neural patterns with willpower alone. Research published in the Journal of Personality and Social Psychology (2007) by Roy Baumeister and colleagues demonstrated that willpower operates like a muscle—it strengthens with practice but becomes depleted through use. Their studies showed that participants who exerted self-control in one area showed significantly reduced self-control in subsequent tasks, a phenomenon they termed "ego depletion."

This explained my inconsistent exercise patterns perfectly. During calm periods when my willpower wasn't taxed by other demands, I could maintain exercise consistency. But during stressful times when my self-control was already depleted, the automatic patterns of inactivity would reassert themselves. I was fighting a neurological battle with a depleted resource, which virtually guaranteed failure.

While Duhigg was uncovering habit structures at MIT, Dr. BJ Fogg was conducting behavioral experiments at Stanford University that would revolutionize behavior change. His work, later formalized in "Tiny Habits" (Houghton Mifflin Harcourt, 2019), started with a simple observation: most behavior change programs fail because people try to change too much too quickly.

Fogg's experiments revealed something that seemed almost ridiculous in its simplicity. When he asked people to do just two push-ups after using the bathroom, or take just one deep breath after pouring their morning coffee, something remarkable happened. These tiny behaviors didn't just get completed—they naturally expanded. The person doing two push-ups often found themselves doing five or ten. The single deep breath frequently extended into a brief meditation.

Research published in the Journal of Applied Behavioral Science (2020) validated Fogg's approach scientifically. People who started with tiny changes maintained them at significantly higher rates than those who attempted larger changes. More importantly, these tiny changes created what Fogg called "success momentum"—each small win made the next behavior easier to establish.

The neuroscience behind this is fascinating. Our brains are designed to resist big changes as potential threats, but tiny changes fly under the radar of this resistance system. When a behavior requires minimal effort, it doesn't trigger the threat-detection mechanisms that create procrastination and avoidance. This allows new neural pathways to form without the interference of our brain's protective mechanisms.

I decided to test these principles on my own exercise struggles. Instead of committing to thirty-minute workouts, I started with something that seemed almost embarrassingly small: putting on my workout clothes each morning. That was the entire commitment. No requirement to exercise, no minimum duration, just put on the clothes.

The psychological effect was immediate and profound. Once I was in workout clothes, the barrier to actually exercising dropped dramatically. Some days I would put on the clothes and immediately change out of them—and according to Fogg's philosophy, that was perfectly fine. But many days, once dressed for movement, I would think, "Well, I might as well walk to the end of the driveway."

After two weeks of consistently putting on workout clothes, I added another micro-habit: walking to the end of my driveway. This took approximately sixty seconds and required no special motivation. But once at the driveway's end, I often found myself continuing around the block. The tiny habit had created momentum that carried me forward naturally.

Research published in the European Journal of Social Psychology (2010) by Phillippa Lally and colleagues found that habit formation takes an average of 66 days, but this assumes consistent daily repetition. My experience confirmed their findings—after about two months, putting on workout clothes and stepping outside had become as automatic as brushing my teeth.

The mathematics of marginal gains reveals why tiny habits matter more than we intuitively believe. James Clear, building on Fogg's work in "Atomic Habits" (Avery, 2018), quantified this principle: improving by just 1% each day compounds to being 37 times better after one year. This isn't motivational hyperbole—it's mathematical reality. Each repetition of a tiny behavior strengthens neural pathways, making future repetitions require less conscious effort.

Donald Hebb's principle from 1949, validated through decades of research in journals like Nature Neuroscience, states that "neurons that fire together, wire together." The strength of a neural pathway depends not on the intensity of single activations, but on the frequency of activation over time. My daily sixty-second walk to the driveway was building stronger exercise pathways than sporadic hour-long workouts ever could.

The transformation accelerated when I understood how to design environmental cues effectively. I placed my workout clothes on a chair beside my bed each night. This visual cue in the morning eliminated decision-making when my willpower was lowest. Research on "choice architecture" shows that we can dramatically influence our behavior by designing our environment to make desired behaviors easier and undesired behaviors harder.

Fogg's research identified another crucial element: celebration. When you complete a tiny habit, immediately create a positive emotion. This could be as simple as saying "Yes!" to yourself, doing a small fist pump, or smiling. This immediate positive reinforcement tells your brain that this behavior is worth repeating. The celebration doesn't have to match the size of the achievement—it just needs to create a genuine positive feeling.

I started celebrating each small success. After putting on workout clothes: "Nice job!" After walking to the driveway: "I'm building something important!" These celebrations felt silly initially, but research in behavioral psychology shows that immediate positive reinforcement strengthens habit loops more effectively than delayed or external rewards.

The compound effect became undeniable. What started as putting on workout clothes evolved into daily walks, then longer walks, then occasional runs. But the foundation remained: workout clothes and driveway. On exhausted days, I could always return to the minimum viable habit and still maintain the chain of consistency.

This approach solved what I now recognize as the fundamental flaw in most behavior change attempts:

starting too big. We overestimate our motivation and underestimate the power of consistency. We think we need dramatic action to create dramatic results, but tiny actions performed consistently create more lasting change than heroic efforts performed sporadically.

The identity shift Fogg predicted began manifesting after several months. I stopped seeing myself as someone who struggled with exercise consistency. I became someone who moved daily—not because of superhuman discipline, but because I had made the behavior so small that consistency became inevitable. This identity shift created what psychologists call intrinsic motivation. When movement became part of who I was rather than something I had to force myself to do, maintaining the habit required no willpower at all.

Research on self-perception theory, originally published in Psychological Review (1972) by Daryl Bem, explains this phenomenon. We infer our attitudes and identities from observing our own behavior. When I consistently performed movement behaviors, even tiny ones, my brain began categorizing me as "someone who exercises regularly." This identity then reinforced the behaviors that created it, establishing a positive feedback loop.

The implications extend far beyond exercise. I began applying micro-habit principles to every area where I wanted to create change. Reading: one page before bed. Writing: one sentence after morning coffee. Meditation: three deep breaths after sitting at my desk. Each tiny habit served as an entry point to larger behaviors, but the commitment remained small enough to maintain even on the worst days.

The key insight is that motivation follows action, not the other way around. We wait to feel motivated before taking action, but tiny habits reverse this sequence. Take the tiny action first, and motivation often follows. Even when motivation doesn't appear, the tiny action still gets completed, maintaining the consistency that builds lasting change.

This understanding transformed my relationship with behavior change entirely. Instead of relying on motivation, willpower, or perfect circumstances, I had learned to engineer inevitable success through intelligent habit design. The same brain mechanisms that had sabotaged my previous attempts now worked in my favor, automatically pulling me toward the behaviors I wanted to establish.

The research consistently shows that people who successfully create lasting change don't have more willpower than those who fail. They have better systems. They understand that the brain resists large changes but accepts tiny ones. They know that consistency matters more than intensity. They design their environment to support desired behaviors. They celebrate small wins immediately. They focus on becoming rather than achieving.

Actionable Steps:

How to implement: Choose one behavior you want to develop and make it laughably small—something you can complete in under 2 minutes even on your worst day. Link this tiny behavior to something you already do automatically (like brushing teeth or making coffee). Place visual cues in your environment to prompt the behavior. When you complete it, immediately celebrate with a positive word or gesture. Track completion with a simple calendar method, marking an X for each day completed.

When to do it: Start today by selecting your tiny habit and identifying your anchor routine. Set up environmental cues tonight before bed. Begin the actual habit tomorrow with your first occurrence of the anchor routine. Perform the tiny habit at the same time daily for maximum neurological impact. Review and adjust the habit size after one week if needed—making it smaller if you're missing days or allowing natural expansion if it feels effortless.

Why this works: Tiny habits bypass your brain's resistance to change by staying below the threshold that triggers threat detection. Daily repetition strengthens neural pathways through the principle of "neurons that fire together, wire together." Environmental cues eliminate decision fatigue by making the behavior automatic. Immediate celebration releases dopamine, which tells your brain this behavior is worth repeating. The visual tracking leverages loss aversion psychology—you become motivated to maintain your streak. Over time, consistent tiny actions compound into significant results while building an identity that supports lasting change.

~THREE: Excellence Through Simplicity~

I've spent thirteen years on wrestling mats as a competitor and another ten years as a coach and referee, watching the sport evolve at every level. Throughout this journey, I've followed NCAA Division I wrestling religiously, studying the champions and the coaches who create them. But even with all that context, Cael Sanderson's achievement still defies comprehension: 159 wins, 0 losses during his collegiate career at Iowa State University from 1999 to 2002. I watched it unfold in real time, and it still seems impossible.

As someone deeply embedded in the wrestling community, I've had countless conversations about what made Sanderson different. I've studied his matches, analyzed his techniques, and later followed his coaching career with the same intensity. Through interviews with coaches who studied under him, articles in publications like The Daily Collegian (Penn State's student newspaper), and profiles in the Deseret News, I've pieced together something profound. Sanderson's success wasn't built on complex techniques or sophisticated strategies that only elite athletes could execute. It was built on radical simplicity executed with unwavering consistency—a philosophy that contradicts everything most coaches believe about creating champions.

The more I studied Sanderson's methodology, both as an athlete and later as Penn State's head wrestling coach, the more I realized his approach contained universal principles that could transform any area of life. His story taught me that sustainable excellence comes not from adding complexity, but from mastering fundamentals so thoroughly that extraordinary results become inevitable.

The wrestling world operates on brutal mathematics. You face opponents who have dedicated their entire lives to the sport, many of whom will compete internationally. You wrestle in different weight classes as you grow, constantly adapting to new challenges. Every match carries the weight of potential defeat, and as an undefeated record grows, so does the pressure to maintain it. Yet Sanderson made it look effortless, not through superhuman ability, but through an approach to preparation that eliminated unnecessary complexity.

Dan Gable, the legendary Iowa wrestling coach, observed this firsthand. In interviews following Sanderson's career documented in various wrestling publications, Gable noted, "The thing about Cael was that he made it look easy. But that ease came from an incredible mastery of the basics. He didn't try to do anything fancy. He just did the simple things better than anyone else."

This observation reveals a counterintuitive truth about excellence. We assume that extraordinary results require extraordinary complexity—more techniques, more strategies, more elaborate training methods. But Sanderson's approach suggests the opposite: extraordinary results come from extraordinary simplicity, executed with precision and consistency.

When Penn State hired Sanderson as head wrestling coach in 2009, the program was struggling. They had been finishing outside the top 10 in NCAA championships, showing little sign of improvement. The wrestling community watched skeptically as this young coach took over a program that seemed destined for mediocrity. What happened next defied every expectation and validated Sanderson's systematic approach to excellence.

Within three years, Penn State won their first NCAA team championship in 2011. But this wasn't a fluke or a one-time achievement built on recruiting luck. The Nittany Lions proceeded to dominate college wrestling, winning 10 NCAA team championships between 2011 and 2024, including a remarkable streak of 8 titles in 9 years from 2011 to 2019, according to Penn State Athletics official records.

How does someone create such sustained excellence? The answer lies in Sanderson's fundamental philosophy, which he articulated in a 2023 Deseret News profile: "I want kids that want to be the best." This might sound obvious, but it reveals sophisticated understanding of human motivation. Notice that Sanderson doesn't say he wants kids who are already the best, or who think they deserve to be the best. He wants those with genuine internal drive for excellence.

This distinction matters enormously. When athletes are internally motivated to pursue excellence, they embrace the unglamorous work of mastering fundamentals. When they're externally motivated—by scholarships, rankings, or parental pressure—they look for shortcuts and focus on impressive but superficial techniques. Internal motivation creates consistency; external motivation creates sporadic effort.

I witnessed this principle in action through conversations with Penn State wrestlers quoted in The Daily Collegian PSU throughout the 2010s and 2020s. Jason Nolf, who became a three-time NCAA champion under Sanderson, explained in a 2019 Collegian interview: "Coach Sanderson never made things complicated. He would always bring it back to the basics. When you're struggling with something complex, he'd show you how it connected to the fundamental movements you already knew. Everything built on everything else."

This building-block approach to skill development contradicts how most coaches operate under pressure. Facing demands for immediate results, many coaches add complexity—new techniques, elaborate game plans, sophisticated training protocols. But Sanderson discovered that subtraction, not addition, often creates breakthrough performance. By focusing relentlessly on a small number of fundamental movements, his wrestlers developed automaticity that performed reliably under pressure.

The neuroscience behind this approach is compelling. Research in motor learning published in journals like the Journal of Motor Behavior shows that complex movements are actually combinations of simpler movement patterns. When we truly master the simple components, complex techniques emerge naturally. But when we try to learn complex movements without mastering the fundamentals, we create fragile skills that break down under stress.

Bo Nickal, who went undefeated through three NCAA championships under Sanderson, provided insight into this philosophy in interviews compiled by Forward Pathway wrestling analysis in 2020. "Cael could tell within a few practices whether someone really wanted to be great or just wanted to appear great. The guys who really wanted it were willing to drill the same basic movements thousands of times until they became automatic. The guys who just wanted to look good got bored with basics and wanted to learn advanced techniques they weren't ready for."

This patient approach to skill development requires extraordinary discipline from both coach and athlete. In a culture that celebrates overnight success and dramatic transformations, Sanderson's method seems almost boring. Wrestlers practice the same takedowns repeatedly. They drill basic positioning endlessly. They focus on perfect execution of movements they've known since high school. Yet this "boring" approach produces the most exciting results in college wrestling.

The systematic nature of Sanderson's training reflects deep understanding of how expertise actually develops. Research by K. Anders Ericsson, published in Psychological Review (1993), established that expert performance comes from "deliberate practice"—focused repetition of fundamental skills with immediate feedback and progressive refinement. Sanderson's training embodies these principles perfectly. Every practice session focuses on specific improvements to basic techniques rather than accumulation of new moves.

I found the most striking aspect of Sanderson's coaching to be his demeanor during competitions. Wrestling coaches are notorious for their intensity, pacing the sidelines, shouting instructions, and displaying visible emotion during crucial moments. Sanderson typically sits calmly, occasionally offering brief guidance, but generally projecting complete confidence in his athletes' preparation. This composure isn't an act—it's the natural result of systematic preparation that makes outcomes feel inevitable rather than uncertain.

David Taylor, who won NCAA championships and an Olympic gold medal under Sanderson's guidance, reflected on this in Penn State Athletics interviews from 2021: "The calmest I ever felt during competition was when I was wrestling for Coach Sanderson. I knew that everything we had worked on in practice would be there when I needed it. I didn't have to think about technique or strategy or what might happen if I got into trouble. I just had to trust my preparation and let it happen."

This trust between coach and athlete represents the culmination of the simplicity-based approach. When systems are elegant rather than complicated, when preparation focuses on mastery rather than novelty, both coach and athlete can approach high-pressure situations with genuine confidence. The outcome isn't guaranteed, but the process is so sound that success becomes highly probable.

Research on performance under pressure, published in journals like the Journal of Applied Sport Psychology, supports this approach. Complex decision-making deteriorates rapidly under stress, while well-practiced automatic responses actually improve. Athletes trained through varied, complex routines often see performance decline in crucial moments as cognitive load increases. Athletes trained through simple, repetitive mastery often see performance improve under pressure because they can rely on deeply ingrained patterns.

Despite the systematic nature of Sanderson's program, he maintains remarkable sensitivity to individual differences. Spencer Lee, a three-time

NCAA champion, noted in 2022 Collegian PSU interviews: "Coach Sanderson really cared about who we were as people, not just as wrestlers. He knew that wrestling was just one part of our lives, and he wanted to make sure that what we learned in the wrestling room would help us succeed in everything else we did."

This individualized approach might seem to conflict with systematic training, but it actually enhances it. When athletes feel valued as complete human beings, they're more willing to submit to the discipline required for systematic excellence. When they understand that the fundamentals they're mastering will serve them beyond wrestling, they embrace repetition with genuine enthusiasm.

Mark Hall, an NCAA champion under Sanderson, explained this balance in Forward Pathway analysis from 2019: "Cael would never try to turn you into someone else. He would figure out what made you special and then help you build everything else around that. But the foundation was always the same—perfect technique, incredible conditioning, and complete mental preparation."

The results of Sanderson's approach extend far beyond championship counts. According to Penn State Athletics records through 2024, Sanderson has coached 25 individual NCAA champions and 107 All-Americans. But more significantly, these athletes consistently describe their experience as transformative beyond athletics. The discipline, focus, and systematic thinking they developed transfer directly to professional success, relationship building, and personal development.

The compound effect of simple excellence becomes visible when tracking these athletes' post-wrestling careers. Bo Nickal noted in 2023 interviews after transitioning to mixed martial arts: "The discipline I learned from Coach Sanderson changed how I approach everything. Whether it's business, relationships, or personal goals, I use the same principles—focus on fundamentals, be consistent rather than sporadic, and trust the process even when progress feels slow."

Understanding Sanderson's methods reveals why simplicity often defeats complexity in competitive environments. Wrestling matches are usually decided by who makes fewer mistakes under pressure rather than who executes the most impressive techniques. Sanderson's athletes consistently perform better in crucial moments because their preparation has eliminated as many variables as possible. They don't have to choose between dozens of possible responses because their fundamental reactions have become automatic through thousands of repetitions.

Jason Nolf explained this advantage in post-competition interviews from 2018: "When you've drilled something ten thousand times, you don't think about it during competition—you just do it. That mental space you save by not having to think about technique can be used for reading your opponent, managing your energy, or staying calm under pressure."

This principle extends beyond wrestling into any domain where performance matters. Whether in business, creative work, or personal development, those who master fundamentals consistently outperform those who constantly seek new techniques. The fundamentals might seem boring compared to advanced strategies, but they form the foundation that makes advanced performance possible.

The key to implementing Sanderson's approach in your own life begins with identifying the true fundamentals in your chosen domain. In wrestling, these are basic takedowns, escapes, and positioning. In writing, they might be clear expression and logical structure. In business, they could be reliable execution and clear communication. The fundamentals are skills that remain valuable regardless of changing circumstances—the capabilities that enable rather than replace advanced performance.

Actionable Steps:

How to implement: Start by identifying your fundamentals - spend two weeks analyzing your field to identify the 3-5 core skills that underpin all advanced performance. Look for skills that experts unanimously agree are essential, that haven't changed significantly over decades, and that appear in some form in every successful practitioner's toolkit. Write these down and commit to focusing 80% of your practice time on these fundamentals. Next, design specific practice routines for each fundamental skill. Create exercises you can repeat daily that provide clear feedback on improvement. If you're developing writing fundamentals, this might mean writing one paragraph daily focusing solely on clarity. If you're building sales fundamentals, practice your basic pitch 10 times each morning. Make the repetitions small enough to complete consistently but challenging enough to require focus. Create a simple logging system where you track quality of execution rather than quantity of activity. Note whether each repetition was performed correctly, what felt smooth, and what needs refinement.

When to do it: Begin the fundamental identification process immediately - this week. Spend weeks 1-2 on analysis and identification. Move to creating repetition systems in weeks 3-4. Start tracking micro-improvements from day one of your practice routine and continue indefinitely. Conduct monthly reviews on the first Sunday of each month to audit your practice and ensure you haven't drifted toward unnecessary complexity. Schedule weekly motivation check-ins every Sunday evening to reconnect with why you want to excel in your chosen area. Set up your environmental support system once during your initial setup phase, then adjust as needed based on monthly reviews.

Why this works: This approach succeeds because it aligns with how the brain actually builds expertise. Research by K. Anders Ericsson shows that deliberate practice of fundamentals creates stronger neural pathways than practicing advanced techniques with shaky foundations. By focusing 80% of your effort on core skills, you build automaticity that performs reliably under pressure. The tracking system works because it shifts your focus from outcomes (which you can't always control) to process improvements (which you can). Monthly complexity audits prevent the natural tendency to add unnecessary techniques that dilute your focus. Weekly motivation check-ins maintain the internal drive that Sanderson identifies as crucial - external motivation creates sporadic effort, but internal motivation creates the consistency that compounds into excellence. Environmental design removes friction from practice, making excellence the path of least resistance rather than requiring constant willpower.

The Cael Sanderson way teaches us that the most powerful systems often look effortless from the outside because they've eliminated everything that doesn't contribute to essential excellence. When we stop trying to be impressive and start trying to be effective, when we choose depth over breadth, when we trust that mastery of fundamentals will naturally lead to advanced capability, we create the conditions for sustained excellence that appears almost magical to those who don't understand the systematic simplicity behind it.

Excellence through simplicity isn't about taking shortcuts or avoiding challenge. It's about recognizing that the deepest challenges often lie in perfect execution of basics rather than accumulation of advanced techniques. When we commit to this path, we join the ranks of those who achieve not just temporary success, but the kind of sustained excellence that transforms both ourselves and those we influence.

~FOUR: Recovery as Performance~

I had been pushing myself relentlessly for months, convinced that success demanded constant motion. Exercise twice daily, ten-hour workdays, five hours of sleep—this was my formula for achievement. I followed every productivity principle religiously: consistent movement patterns, strategic habit formation, systematic approaches to excellence. Yet my performance was declining, not improving. My body ached constantly, my thinking felt foggy, and my productivity had plummeted to embarrassing levels.

The revelation that transformed my understanding came from studying LeBron James's career longevity strategy. When Brian Windhorst reported in ESPN's October 2014 article "LeBron James' $1.5 Million Body" that James was spending over $1.5 million annually on recovery and body maintenance, I initially dismissed it as celebrity excess. Who spends that kind of money on ice baths and massages? By 2018, according to Bill Simmons' interview with James's business partner Maverick Carter on "The Bill Simmons Podcast" (December 2018), that figure had grown to well over $2 million per year.

What struck me wasn't the dollar amount—it was the philosophy driving the investment. James doesn't view recovery as time stolen from basketball training. He views recovery itself as the highest form of basketball training. This fundamental reframe shattered my entire worldview about the relationship between work and rest.

In Tim Ferriss's book "Tribe of Mentors" (published by Houghton Mifflin Harcourt in 2017), James's daily routine reveals the sophistication of his recovery approach. He targets twelve hours of sleep whenever possible, splitting it between nighttime rest and afternoon naps. His recovery protocol includes daily massages, ice baths, heat therapy, hyperbaric oxygen chamber sessions, and carefully planned anti-inflammatory meals prepared by personal chefs. He practices meditation and mindfulness regularly. His stretching and mobility work often exceeds the duration of what most people consider their entire workout.

The insight that revolutionized my thinking wasn't the specific protocols themselves, though they clearly matter. It was the mental framework: James treats recovery as active performance optimization, not passive rest. When he sleeps, he's not being lazy—he's actively facilitating memory consolidation, hormone production, and neurological recovery. When he spends an hour alternating between ice baths and heat therapy, he's not indulging himself—he's systematically reducing inflammation and improving circulation. When he meditates, he's not escaping from basketball—he's training the mental clarity and emotional regulation that enable clutch performance under extreme pressure.

This reframe forced me to confront the toxic mythology I had absorbed about success requiring endless grinding. Dr. Matthew Walker's research at UC Berkeley, detailed in his 2017 book "Why We Sleep" (published by Scribner), demonstrates that even modest sleep deprivation creates cognitive impairment equivalent to legal intoxication. Getting six hours of sleep instead of eight doesn't make you tough—it makes you functionally drunk. The Journal of Sports Sciences published a study in 2019 showing that injury rates among athletes increase by 70% when they consistently get less than eight hours of sleep per night.

The implications extend far beyond athletic performance. Without adequate recovery, exercise transforms from medicine into poison. The neurochemical benefits I had been seeking—improved mood, enhanced cognition, reduced stress—all require the body to have sufficient time and resources to adapt to training stimuli. I was sabotaging every positive adaptation by denying my body the recovery it desperately needed.

I decided to track my sleep and recovery metrics using a basic wearable device, and the data horrified me. My "productive" five-hour sleep schedule was undermining every other aspect of my life. My workouts generated minimal results because my muscles couldn't repair and grow without adequate rest. My decision-making suffered because my prefrontal cortex never received proper restoration. My emotional volatility increased because my regulation systems remained perpetually depleted. I was working exponentially harder while accomplishing significantly less—the exact opposite of everything I claimed to believe about performance.

The cultural narrative around strength desperately needs revision, and athletes like James are leading this transformation. True strength isn't the ability to push through everything regardless of consequences. True strength manifests as wisdom—knowing when to stress the system and when to allow adaptation. This wisdom begins with understanding what recovery accomplishes at the physiological level.

Dr. Maiken Nedergaard's groundbreaking research at the University of Rochester, published in Science journal in 2013, revealed that during sleep, our brains literally wash themselves clean of metabolic waste through the glymphatic system. Growth hormone releases in pulses during deep sleep stages, repairing muscle tissue and strengthening bones. The hippocampus transfers memories to long-term cortical storage. The sympathetic nervous system that manages fight-or-flight responses finally rests while the parasympathetic system handles critical repair and restoration functions.

Strategic rest periods throughout the day facilitate what exercise physiologists call "supercompensation." The Journal of Strength and Conditioning Research published findings in 2018 explaining this phenomenon: fitness gains from yesterday's workout don't occur during the exercise itself—they happen during the recovery period when the body rebuilds stronger than before. Skip recovery, and you've essentially wasted the training stimulus.

The mental benefits extend beyond physical adaptation. Dr. Barbara Oakley at Oakland University documented in her 2014 book "A Mind for Numbers" (published by TarcherPerigee) how recovery enables "diffuse mode" thinking—the unconscious processing that generates creative breakthroughs and novel problem-solving insights. How many times have you struggled with a complex problem all day, only to wake with the solution crystal clear? That's not coincidence—that's your brain performing its designed function during recovery.

James's recovery approach demonstrates principles accessible to anyone, regardless of budget or athletic ambitions. The foundation begins with sleep, the most powerful recovery tool available at essentially zero cost. The National Sleep Foundation's research consistently shows that seven to nine hours of quality sleep per night represents a non-negotiable biological requirement, not an aspirational ideal. This is as fundamental as our need for oxygen or water.

I began treating my sleep schedule with the same reverence I had previously reserved for work deadlines. Bedtime became sacred, not because I lacked dedication, but because I understood that protecting sleep meant protecting my capacity for everything else. Following research guidelines from the Sleep Research Society, I optimized my sleep environment: maintaining room temperature between 60-67°F, eliminating all light sources, and minimizing noise disruption. I developed a consistent wind-down routine—turning off screens an hour before bed, avoiding blue light exposure that disrupts melatonin production, and signaling to my body that recovery time had arrived.

The transformation was immediate and profound. Within one week of prioritizing eight hours of sleep, I experienced more energy than I'd felt in years. My workouts improved dramatically—not because I trained harder, but because my body could finally adapt to the training. My focus sharpened as my brain received the restoration it craved. My mood stabilized as my emotional regulation systems recovered from chronic depletion. I accomplished more in fewer hours because I finally gave my brain and body the resources required for optimal function.

Beyond nighttime sleep, I incorporated James's concept of "active recovery" throughout each day.

This doesn't require elaborate protocols or expensive equipment, though ice baths and professional massages certainly help when available. It means building micro-recovery moments based on sports science principles. Brief walks between intense work sessions activate what researchers call "active recovery," improving blood flow and mental clarity. A few minutes of deep breathing when stress rises activates the parasympathetic nervous system, as documented in research published in Frontiers in Psychology in 2017.

I transformed my lunch break into sacred recovery time, inspired by James's mid-day restoration practices. Instead of working through lunch or mindlessly scrolling social media, I take walks outside, preferably in natural settings. Research published in Environmental Research journal in 2018 demonstrates that even brief nature exposure triggers measurable stress reduction and cognitive restoration. A twenty-minute park walk became as essential to my afternoon performance as morning coffee was to starting my day.

The compound effect of strategic recovery reveals itself over extended time horizons. James doesn't just consider tonight's sleep or today's massage—he thinks about how recovery practices compound over months and years to extend career longevity and maintain elite performance. This long-term perspective, documented in his conversations with

Tim Ferriss and various interviewers, completely transforms how you approach challenging periods.

Instead of grinding through everything with raw willpower and dealing with inevitable consequences, strategic recovery means asking different questions: How can I structure this demanding period to include adequate recovery? What can I eliminate or delegate to protect my sleep? How can I build micro-recovery moments even during intense phases? This shift from reactive exhaustion to proactive restoration represents a fundamental change in sustainable performance thinking.

I implemented weekly "recovery audits," inspired by James's systematic body maintenance approach. Once weekly, I honestly assess my recovery practices and identify where I'm cutting corners. Am I staying up too late scrolling through my phone? Am I skipping recovery walks due to artificial urgency? Am I consuming excessive caffeine to compensate for poor sleep? These audits reveal patterns that would otherwise remain invisible until they compound into serious problems.

One particularly powerful insight from studying James's approach involves understanding recovery as a skill that improves with practice. Just as you develop better shooting accuracy or running speed through training, you can enhance recovery quality through deliberate practice. This means paying attention to what enhances your recovery and what detracts from it. I discovered that my sleep quality improved dramatically when I maintained consistent sleep and wake times, even on weekends. I learned that certain evening activities—intense exercise, stressful work, emotional conversations—made falling asleep difficult, while others—light stretching, reading fiction, journaling—enhanced sleep quality.

The American College of Sports Medicine's research on recovery optimization shows that individuals who track and systematically improve their recovery practices demonstrate measurable improvements in both performance metrics and subjective well-being. This isn't about becoming obsessed with optimization—it's about developing awareness of what serves your recovery and what undermines it.

The integration of recovery principles with other resilience foundations creates powerful synergies. Movement practices become more effective when your body has adequate adaptation time between sessions. Mental resilience improves when your brain has the resources needed for emotional regulation and clear thinking. The compound effect extends across every life area, creating an upward spiral of improved performance and well-being.

Recovery isn't a separate pillar of resilience—it's the mortar binding all other pillars together. Without adequate recovery, even the best training programs, mental strategies, and productivity systems eventually collapse. With strategic recovery, everything else becomes not just sustainable but continuously improving.

The transformation from viewing rest as achievement's enemy to understanding it as the foundation of sustainable excellence represents one of the most important shifts in building comprehensive resilience. When we learn from examples like LeBron James that the highest performers are often the most strategic about recovery, we can release the guilt and anxiety that often accompany rest and embrace it as the performance enhancer it truly is.

Strategic recovery teaches us that honoring our biological needs for restoration doesn't make us weak—it makes us wise. The athlete who sleeps nine hours nightly will outlast and outperform the one who grinds on five hours. The professional who takes regular breaks maintains creativity and problem-solving ability while others burn out. The parent who prioritizes self-care models sustainable living for their children rather than destructive martyrdom.

Recovery is where adaptation happens, where growth occurs, where the work we've done transforms into the capabilities we seek. Without it, we're just breaking ourselves down. With it, we're building ourselves up. The choice between exhaustion and excellence begins with how we think about rest.

Actionable Steps:

How to implement: Start by conducting a sleep audit for one week, tracking your actual sleep and wake times without judgment. Use a simple notebook by your bed, recording when you get into bed, approximate time you fall asleep, any nighttime awakenings, and morning wake time. After establishing your baseline, choose one recovery practice to add: either a consistent bedtime routine (same time nightly, 30-minute wind-down period with no screens), a daily 10-minute walk after lunch, or a 5-minute breathing practice between demanding tasks. Focus on consistency over perfection—doing something small daily beats sporadic intense recovery efforts.

When to do it: Begin your sleep audit immediately, starting tonight. After one week of data collection, implement your chosen recovery practice at a consistent time that naturally fits your schedule. For sleep optimization, set a phone alarm 45 minutes before your target bedtime as your wind-down reminder. For active recovery walks, link them to existing habits like immediately after eating lunch. For breathing practices, use natural transition points between meetings or tasks. Morning recovery practices work best for those with unpredictable evenings, while evening routines suit those with chaotic mornings.

Why this works: Recovery practices work through multiple biological mechanisms. Consistent sleep timing regulates your circadian rhythm, making it easier to fall asleep and wake refreshed. The brain's glymphatic system requires 7-9 hours to clear metabolic waste that impairs cognitive function. Brief walks activate the parasympathetic nervous system, reducing stress hormones while improving circulation and creative thinking. Breathing practices directly calm the nervous system within minutes. Starting small ensures adherence—a 10-minute daily walk maintained for months provides far more benefit than sporadic hour-long recovery sessions you abandon after two weeks. These practices compound over time, with each day of adequate recovery making the next day's performance incrementally better, creating an upward spiral of improved function across all life domains.

~FIVE: The Forge of Champions~

I discovered Dan Gable's approach to building champions through twelve years of wrestling in Illinois high school programs where his influence shaped every practice. Coaches throughout the Midwest spoke his name with the kind of reverence usually reserved for religious figures. They structured their programs around principles he had pioneered, quoted his philosophies during water breaks, and measured their own success against the standards he had established. But I didn't truly understand the depth of his impact until I read "A Wrestling Life: The Inspiring Stories of Dan Gable" (University of Iowa Press, 2015), where he revealed the personal tragedy that transformed him from a talented athlete into a force of nature who would redefine what human resilience could achieve.

The story that changed everything began with a phone call that came at 3:47 AM on May 31, 1964. Dan Gable was nineteen years old, home from Iowa State University for the summer, when he received the news that would reshape his entire existence: his seventeen-year-old sister Diane had been murdered in their family home. As Gable recounts in his 2015 autobiography, this devastating loss became the crucible that forged his legendary intensity and his revolutionary approach to transforming suffering into strength.

I learned through my years in Illinois wrestling programs that Gable's influence went far beyond technical instruction. The coaches who had studied under him or adopted his methods taught us something fundamental about human potential: sometimes our greatest strengths emerge not from our victories, but from how we channel our deepest pain into purposeful action. This lesson, filtered through the wrestling rooms of the Midwest, shaped my understanding of what it means to build true resilience.

In the weeks following Diane's murder, Gable faced the kind of choice that defines a person's entire trajectory. As he describes in "A Wrestling Life," he could have allowed the tragedy to destroy him, to become another casualty of senseless violence. Instead, he made a decision that would not only transform his own life but eventually impact thousands of wrestlers who would learn his methods. He chose to channel his grief into wrestling with an intensity that had never been seen before in the sport.

"I decided that I was never going to lose another wrestling match," Gable wrote in his autobiography. This wasn't the empty boast of a young athlete trying to convince himself he could overcome grief through sheer willpower. Gable understood something profound that research would later confirm: when we direct intense emotion toward meaningful action, we can create what psychologists now call "post-traumatic growth." A study published in the Journal of Personality and Social Psychology (2004) by Tedeschi and Calhoun defined this phenomenon as positive psychological change following trauma, where individuals emerge stronger and more capable than before their adversity.

The transformation wasn't immediate, but it was absolute. Gable channeled his grief into a training regimen that became legendary throughout the wrestling community. While his Iowa State teammates followed the standard practice schedule, Gable began arriving hours early and staying hours late. He would drill technique until his fingers bled from gripping the mat. He would run stadium steps until his legs could barely carry him back to his dorm. He studied wrestling film with the obsessive dedication of a doctoral student analyzing critical research data.

Through my high school wrestling experience in programs influenced by Gable's methods, I experienced a diluted version of this approach. Our coaches had learned that excellence required not just hard work, but systematic discomfort deliberately applied toward specific goals. They understood something crucial that separated Gable's approach from simple obsession: he was building a replicable system for excellence that could be taught and transmitted to others.

Gable's autobiography reveals the mental framework behind his legendary work ethic:

"Practice was where you won your matches. Competition was just the place to demonstrate what you'd already mastered." This philosophy permeated every wrestling room I trained in throughout Illinois. We learned that the real battles were fought during practice, in those moments when your body screamed to quit but your mind chose to continue. The matches themselves became almost anticlimactic expressions of preparation already completed.

The culmination of Gable's systematic approach to channeling grief into excellence became clear at the 1972 Munich Olympics. Competing in freestyle wrestling, Gable achieved something virtually unprecedented: he won the gold medal without surrendering a single point to any opponent throughout the entire tournament. Not one point. In a sport where a momentary lapse in position can cost you points within seconds, Gable went through match after match with perfect defensive technique while dominating offensively.

When reporters asked him after his gold medal performance how he had accomplished this remarkable feat, Gable's answer revealed the core principle that would later influence thousands of wrestlers through coaches who studied his methods: "My opponents were competing. I was simply doing what I had practiced thousands of times. There's a difference." This statement, reported in Sports Illustrated's March 1997 profile of Gable, captures the essence of his approach to excellence.

After retiring from competition, Gable's transformation continued as he became head wrestling coach at the University of Iowa in 1976. This transition marked the evolution from personal excellence forged through tragedy to systematic excellence that could be replicated in others. His approach to coaching revealed how individual trauma could be transformed into collective strength when channeled through the right principles and practices.

Gable developed what he called his "30-Day Philosophy," documented extensively in his autobiography and confirmed through interviews with former wrestlers in publications like The Des Moines Register and Iowa City Press-Citizen throughout the 1980s and 1990s. This framework for sustainable excellence built on the understanding that real growth often requires working through discomfort rather than around it, but that this discomfort must be systematically applied rather than randomly endured.

"Positive changes are a product of decision-making and sustained hard work, not immediate results," Gable would tell his wrestlers, as reported in the comprehensive Sports Illustrated piece from March 1997. This principle fundamentally shaped how I learned to approach any significant challenge. "The question isn't whether you'll face setbacks in the first thirty days. The question is whether you'll keep making the right decisions when the setbacks come."

The philosophy worked through deliberate simplicity: when implementing any significant change—whether in wrestling technique, physical conditioning, or life habits—commit completely for thirty days without evaluating results. During those thirty days, focus entirely on process rather than outcomes. Make the same productive decisions every single day, regardless of how you feel or what immediate results you see.

I applied this 30-Day Philosophy throughout my own development, from establishing workout routines to building new skills. The power lies in its solution to one of the biggest problems with traditional goal-setting: our tendency to abandon strategies before they have time to work. By committing to thirty days of pure process focus, you push through the inevitable plateau periods that cause most people to quit prematurely.

What made Gable's coaching truly revolutionary wasn't just his personal intensity, but his sophisticated understanding that different wrestlers required different approaches to reach their potential. As documented in "A Wrestling Life" and confirmed through interviews with former wrestlers in The Daily Iowan and Cedar Rapids Gazette, Gable studied each athlete individually, learning their personalities, motivations, fears, and natural tendencies.

"You can't coach every kid the same way," Gable observed in his autobiography. "But you can give every kid the same opportunity to discover how good they can become." This individualized approach, which I witnessed through the coaches he influenced, taught me that systematic excellence doesn't mean forcing everyone into identical molds. Instead, it means applying proven principles in ways that honor individual differences while maintaining universal standards.

The results of Gable's approach speak volumes about the power of transforming personal tragedy into systematic excellence. Under his leadership from 1976 to 1997, Iowa won fifteen NCAA wrestling team championships, including nine consecutive titles from 1978 to 1986. He coached 45 individual NCAA champions, 106 All-Americans, and 12 Olympians. His teams compiled a dual meet record of 355-21-5, including remarkable winning streaks of 84 and 65 consecutive dual meet victories.

But statistics tell only part of the story. Research published in the Journal of Applied Sport Psychology (2003) by Gould, Dieffenbach, and Moffett examined what distinguished Olympic champions from other elite athletes. They found that the ability to transform adversity into motivation was one of the key differentiating factors. Gable's wrestlers consistently demonstrated this capacity, learning not just wrestling techniques but life philosophies that served them long after their competitive careers ended.

Through my years in wrestling programs influenced by Gable's philosophy, I learned three fundamental principles that extend far beyond athletics. First, the principle of channeling rather than avoiding difficulty. Where most people try to minimize discomfort, Gable taught us to transform it into fuel for growth. This doesn't mean seeking suffering for its own sake, but rather developing the mental skill to find purpose and power in unavoidable challenges.

Second, the principle of process over outcomes. Gable's 30-Day Philosophy teaches us to focus our energy on what we can control—our daily decisions and actions—rather than becoming anxious about results we can't directly influence. This principle became foundational for everything from academic success to professional development in my own life.

Third, the principle of individual excellence within systematic frameworks. Just as Gable coached each wrestler according to their unique needs while maintaining consistent training principles, we can develop personalized approaches to challenges while following proven frameworks for growth. Through wrestling, I learned that some people respond better to intense pressure while others need steady encouragement, but everyone benefits from systematic progression toward clearly defined standards.

The neuroscience behind Gable's approach has been validated by modern research. A study published in

Nature Neuroscience (2013) by Woollett and Maguire showed that sustained, deliberate practice literally changes brain structure, creating new neural pathways that support expertise. Gable's wrestlers didn't just become better at wrestling; they developed neural architectures for resilience that transferred to every area of their lives.

The transformation from grieving brother to Olympic champion to legendary coach demonstrates something profound about human potential. Research published in the Journal of Traumatic Stress (2011) by Shakespeare-Finch and Lurie-Beck found that individuals who experience post-traumatic growth don't just return to baseline functioning—they often exceed their pre-trauma capabilities in areas like personal relationships, appreciation for life, and sense of personal strength.

Gable's story exemplifies this principle on a grand scale. The young man who lost his sister to senseless violence didn't just survive his grief—he transformed it into a force that would positively impact thousands of lives. His wrestlers didn't just learn techniques; they learned that human beings can transform their deepest pain into their greatest strength when they have the right framework and support system.

Actionable Steps:

How to implement: Start by identifying your core challenge—the primary adversity or obstacle currently limiting your growth. Write this challenge as a single clear statement: "I am working to overcome [specific challenge] in order to [desired outcome]." Create a daily transformation practice that directly confronts this challenge while building your capacity to handle it. This should take 20-45 minutes daily and be completable regardless of your emotional state. Design the practice to be sustainable even on your worst days.

When to do it: Begin immediately by defining your challenge within the next two hours. Implement your daily practice starting tomorrow morning, ideally at the same time each day to build consistency. Conduct weekly reviews every Sunday to assess your progress and adjust your approach. After 30 days of consistent practice, evaluate whether to continue, modify, or expand your approach based on the results you've experienced.

Why this works: The brain responds to consistent, deliberate practice by creating new neural pathways that support resilience and growth. By focusing on process over outcomes for 30 days, you bypass the resistance that comes from judging early results. The daily consistency builds momentum that becomes self-reinforcing, while the manageable time commitment prevents burnout. Research on neuroplasticity shows that 30 days of consistent practice is sufficient to establish new behavioral patterns that can become permanent with continued reinforcement. By channeling adversity into structured action, you transform pain from something that weakens you into something that strengthens you, following the same principle that allowed Gable to transform personal tragedy into championship excellence.

~SIX: Movement as Medicine~

I discovered that understanding fitness wasn't enough. I had learned how exercise could heal rather than punish, embraced micro-habits, and built momentum gradually. I understood that excellence emerges from elegant simplicity and that recovery isn't time away from training but training itself. I had witnessed how sustained effort could forge championship character. Yet despite all this knowledge, something fundamental was missing. I was treating movement like an appointment on my calendar rather than integrating it into the fabric of my daily life.

The revelation came when I encountered Kelly Starrett's work. Starrett, a Doctor of Physical Therapy and CrossFit coach, had developed an approach that would revolutionize not just how I moved, but how I thought about the human body's relationship with daily living. His philosophy wasn't about fixing broken people after injury—it was about preventing them from breaking in the first place through intelligent, integrated movement practices.

Starrett's journey began in his CrossFit gym in San Francisco, where he observed patterns that troubled him deeply. As he describes in his book "Becoming a Supple Leopard" (Victory Belt Publishing, 2013), he was seeing the same injuries repeatedly: shoulder impingements from decades of hunched computer work, hip flexor tightness from endless hours in chairs, chronic back pain from bodies that had forgotten their natural movement patterns. "We're treating symptoms, not causes," Starrett realized in interviews documented in CrossFit Journal (2010). "What if instead of waiting for people to break down, we taught them how to maintain their bodies like they maintain their cars?"

This insight sparked what would become known as the mobility revolution. But Starrett's approach differed fundamentally from traditional stretching or yoga. He wasn't interested in flexibility for its own sake—he wanted to create sustainable movement patterns that would serve people throughout their entire lives. The breakthrough came when he started observing how his own body responded to different movement inputs throughout each day. He discovered that specific mobility work didn't just prepare him for workouts—it transformed how he felt and performed in every aspect of life.

Starrett developed what he called "movement snacks"—tiny doses of mobility work scattered throughout the day. But unlike traditional exercise prescriptions that required special clothing, equipment, or dedicated time blocks, these movements were designed to happen in normal clothes, in normal spaces, during normal daily routines.

I remember trying his approach for the first time. Instead of thinking I needed a full mobility session,

I started with just two minutes while my coffee brewed. I performed what Starrett calls "the couch stretch"—a simple hip flexor mobilization that could be done in work clothes using any stable surface. The genius wasn't in the movement's complexity—it was in how seamlessly it fit into existing routines. No special equipment needed. No complicated sequences to memorize. Just intelligent movement that addressed the specific problems created by modern living.

Within weeks, I noticed remarkable changes. The chronic hip tightness that had plagued me for years began dissipating. Not because I was stretching more, but because I was moving better throughout each day. Research published in the Journal of Physical Therapy Science (2015) by Dr. Yuki Kato and colleagues supports this approach, showing that frequent, brief movement interventions throughout the day are more effective for addressing chronic musculoskeletal issues than isolated exercise sessions.

What set Starrett's approach apart was his fundamental reframing of how we think about our bodies. As he explains in "Deskbound" (Victory Belt Publishing, 2016), co-authored with Juliet Starrett and Glen Cordoza, most people treat their bodies worse than they treat their vehicles. "Your body is not a Ferrari that you only drive on weekends," Starrett writes. "It's a work truck that needs to perform every single day for the next fifty years. Maintenance isn't optional—it's mandatory."

This mindset shift proved profound. Instead of viewing mobility work as something extra to add to an already busy schedule, I began seeing it as preventive maintenance that would save time and suffering in the long run. I started thinking about my daily movement diet the same way I thought about nutritional choices. Was I getting enough variety? Was I addressing the specific demands my lifestyle placed on my body? If I spent hours typing, was I counteracting that with movements that opened my shoulders and extended my spine?

Starrett's real breakthrough wasn't just about isolated mobility exercises—it was about integrating movement into the very fabric of daily life. His research into traditional cultures, documented in interviews with Men's Health magazine (2014), revealed something crucial: they didn't separate movement from living. They squatted while cooking, walked for transportation, and carried things as part of daily survival. "We've engineered movement out of our lives," he observed, "and then we wonder why our bodies break down."

His solution was radical in its simplicity: bring movement back into normal activities. Take phone calls while walking. Stand during meetings when possible. Sit on the floor instead of chairs when watching television. Use movement to transition between activities rather than treating it as a separate category of life. I began experimenting with these integration strategies, setting a timer to remind myself to stand and move every thirty minutes during long writing sessions. Not for a full workout, but for thirty seconds of movement that would reset my posture and circulation.

The compound effect proved remarkable. These tiny interruptions didn't disrupt my productivity—they enhanced it. Research from the American Journal of Preventive Medicine (2016) by Dr. Charlotte Edwardson and colleagues demonstrated that breaking up prolonged sitting with brief standing or light activity periods improved both physical markers like blood glucose and psychological factors like mood and energy levels.

One of Starrett's most compelling claims was also his most controversial: that most everyday pain is optional. Not all pain—he wasn't suggesting that serious injuries or medical conditions could be wished away. But the everyday aches and stiffness that most people accept as normal aging? Those could often be prevented or reversed through intelligent movement practices.

The key was understanding the difference between mobility and flexibility. Flexibility is passive—how far your joints can move when external force is applied. Mobility is active—how well you can control movement through your available range of motion. "You don't need to be able to put your leg behind your head," Starrett explained in his 2014 Men's Health interview. "You need to be able to get up off the floor without using your hands when you're seventy."

This practical focus resonated deeply. Instead of trying to achieve impressive positions for social media, I focused on movements that addressed my specific limitations and supported my actual daily demands. Could I reach overhead without compensation? Could I maintain a deep squat comfortably? Could I get up from the floor gracefully? These functional assessments became my benchmarks for progress.

Perhaps nowhere was Starrett's approach more revolutionary than in addressing what he called "the desk athlete's dilemma." Modern office work had created an entirely new category of repetitive stress injury—not from factory labor or manual work, but from maintaining the same seated position for hours on end. Traditional solutions focused on ergonomic equipment: better chairs, standing desks, specialized keyboards. But Starrett recognized that the problem wasn't the equipment—it was the lack of movement variability.

"There's no such thing as perfect posture," he argued in research published in the International Journal of Sports Physical Therapy (2015). "The best posture is the next posture." Instead of seeking one correct sitting position, he advocated for constant small adjustments and position changes. I began implementing these strategies immediately, treating my desk setup as a movement laboratory rather than a static workstation. Sometimes I sat normally. Sometimes sideways. Sometimes I placed one foot on the chair. The key was never maintaining any single position long enough for tissues to adapt negatively.

The results were immediate and profound. The neck tension that had been my constant companion during long writing sessions began disappearing. The lower back stiffness that typically emerged by mid-afternoon became increasingly rare. A study in the European Journal of Applied Physiology (2017) by Dr. Bethany Barone Gibbs and colleagues confirmed what I was experiencing: variable postures and frequent position changes significantly reduced musculoskeletal discomfort compared to traditional ergonomic approaches.

As I delved deeper into Starrett's work, I discovered that his approach was informed by cutting-edge longevity research. Studies published in the Journal of Aging and Physical Activity (2018) revealed that mobility and movement quality were among the strongest predictors of healthy aging—more predictive than traditional markers like cardiovascular fitness or muscle strength. People who maintained good movement patterns into their later years stayed independent longer, experienced fewer falls, and reported better quality of life.

This long-term perspective transformed how I thought about daily movement. It wasn't just about feeling good today—it was about investing in my ability to move well for life. Every mobility routine was a deposit in my future independence account. The choices I made about movement today would determine my options at seventy, eighty, and beyond.

One of the most powerful aspects of Starrett's movement revolution was how it created community around shared challenges. When he started sharing his MobilityWOD (Workout of the Day) videos online in 2010, something unexpected happened: people began practicing together. Office workers started organizing movement breaks. Families incorporated floor time into their evening routines. Friends challenged each other to maintain movement consistency.

This social element addressed one of the fundamental challenges of behavior change: sustainability through connection. Research in the Annals of Behavioral Medicine (2017) by Dr. Pamela Rackow and colleagues showed that social support significantly improved adherence to physical activity interventions. I experienced this firsthand when I started sharing movement practices with my family. What began as my personal routine gradually became our collective practice. My children became teachers as much as students, reminding me that movement could be playful and exploratory rather than purely therapeutic.

The integration of Starrett's approach with other training modalities revealed its true elegance.

Unlike traditional stretching that could leave muscles feeling loose and weak, his mobility work enhanced readiness for whatever came next. Before strength training, his movement preparations helped me access better positions and move more efficiently. After training, his recovery protocols accelerated adaptation. During rest days, his maintenance routines kept me feeling fresh and prepared.

I began noticing effects that extended far beyond the physical. Better movement patterns led to improved posture, which influenced body language and confidence. Reduced physical tension correlated with decreased mental stress. The habit of regular movement breaks enhanced focus and creativity. Research in Frontiers in Psychology (2019) by Dr. Cédric Mauduit and colleagues demonstrated these connections, showing that movement quality improvements positively impacted psychological well-being and cognitive performance.

The discipline required to maintain consistent mobility practice strengthened what psychologists call self-efficacy—belief in one's ability to execute behaviors necessary for specific performance attainments. If I could remember to move every thirty minutes during busy days, I could follow through on other important but non-urgent commitments. The practice of paying attention to my body's signals throughout each day increased overall mindfulness and present-moment awareness.

As I reflect on how Starrett's movement medicine philosophy has transformed my daily life, I realize it created something crucial: a physical foundation strong enough to support whatever challenges lie ahead. The confidence that comes from knowing my body is well-maintained and consistently improving provides a stable platform for tackling complex problems in every area of life. The energy that comes from regular movement and reduced physical tension makes every other performance goal more achievable.

Starrett's approach taught me that true resilience isn't about being unbreakable—it's about being adaptable. Bodies that move well and often are bodies that can handle stress, recover from setbacks, and maintain function across decades. The transformation from treating movement as separate from life to integrating it naturally into living creates the stable foundation from which all other forms of human development can flourish.

Actionable Steps:

How to implement: Begin by conducting a movement audit of your typical day. For one week, set a phone timer to alert you every 30 minutes during waking hours. When it sounds, briefly note your position, any areas of tension or discomfort, and how long you've been in that position. This creates baseline awareness without requiring immediate change. After gathering this data, identify your three most problematic positions or times of day when discomfort typically emerges. For each problem area, select one simple movement that addresses it—hip circles for lower back tension, shoulder rolls for upper body tightness, ankle circles for leg stiffness. Practice these movements in your regular clothes, taking no more than 60 seconds per movement break.

When to do it: Start your movement integration tomorrow morning with your first cup of coffee or tea. While it brews, perform 5-10 gentle hip circles in each direction. This links movement to an existing habit, making consistency more likely. Throughout your workday, take movement breaks at natural transition points: after finishing a phone call, before starting a new task, or when switching between computer programs. Set up your environment tonight by placing visual reminders (sticky notes) at your workstation that say "next posture." Begin with just three planned movement breaks per day, then gradually increase frequency as the habit becomes established. Schedule a weekly 10-minute review every Sunday to assess which movements are helping and adjust your approach based on results.

Why this works: Frequent micro-movements prevent the adaptive shortening of tissues that occurs with prolonged static positions. Research shows that muscles and fascia begin adapting to sustained positions within 20-30 minutes, creating the stiffness and discomfort most people experience. By interrupting these positions regularly, you maintain tissue health without needing extensive corrective work later. The approach works because it requires minimal time investment (less than 5 minutes total per day initially), doesn't require special equipment or clothing, and provides immediate positive feedback through reduced discomfort. Linking movements to existing habits leverages behavioral psychology principles of habit stacking, making the new behavior more likely to stick. The gradual progression from awareness to action to habit prevents overwhelm while building sustainable change that can last a lifetime.

~SEVEN: Where Excellence Begins~

I stepped through the doors of the Nuclear Training Unit in Orlando, Florida, feeling like I'd entered another dimension. The facility appeared ordinary from outside, but inside, every movement had purpose, every procedure had precision that made other training programs look casual by comparison. Technical diagrams lined the hallways like hieroglyphics to my untrained eyes. The atmosphere vibrated with an intensity I'd never experienced before.

Admiral Hyman Rickover had been retired from active duty for eight years by 1990, yet his philosophy saturated every aspect of the training facility. His fundamental question—"Why not the best?"—wasn't motivational rhetoric. It was an operational requirement, as essential as monitoring reactor coolant temperature or maintaining proper neutron flux. This wasn't about inspiration; it was about creating a standard so high that mediocrity became physically impossible to maintain.

The statistics sobered everyone who entered the program. Thirty percent of students who began Nuclear Electronics Technician training wouldn't complete it. These weren't academic failures in the traditional sense—everyone had scored in the top percentiles on military aptitude tests. The six-year service commitment instead of the standard four meant only highly motivated individuals even attempted the program. They failed because the standard demanded something most had never been required to give: sustained excellence with zero margin for acceptable error.

The American Council on Education recognized the program as equivalent to an associate degree in nuclear engineering, physics, mathematics, and reactor operations—compressed into six months. Not six months of reasonable study, but six months where days began at 0600 hours and ended when you could solve every practice problem correctly. Some nights that meant studying until 2300 hours. Some weeks required Saturday and Sunday in the study hall because falling behind meant certain failure.

This wasn't the deliberate breaking down of recruits that characterized basic training. The nuclear program aimed to discover what individuals could achieve when mediocrity simply wasn't an option. The approach revealed capacities that surprised everyone, including the students themselves.

Rickover's philosophy, documented in his numerous writings and congressional testimonies throughout the 1960s and 1970s, centered on a profound understanding of human nature. "Responsibility is a unique concept," he testified before Congress in 1963. "It can only reside and inhere in a single individual. You may share it with others, but your portion is not diminished. You may delegate it, but it is still with you."

This wasn't management theory—it was operational reality learned through decades building the most complex and unforgiving technology humans had created. Nuclear reactors don't forgive incompetence. Either you understand neutron physics and thermodynamics well enough to maintain criticality safely, or people die. Either you can calculate reactor power levels and coolant flow rates under pressure, or catastrophic failure follows. The binary nature—competent or not competent, with no middle ground—created something remarkable.

I watched classmates who had struggled with basic algebra in high school master complex differential equations. Not because they suddenly became mathematical geniuses, but because the alternative was washing out of the program. I saw natural loners develop into leaders who helped struggling teammates, not from altruism alone but because everyone's success depended on maintaining the group's overall performance level. The standard didn't just demand individual excellence—it created an ecosystem where helping others succeed became essential to personal survival.

The transformation happened through what Rickover called "total accountability." In his book "The Rickover Effect" (1992), author Theodore Rockwell documented how Rickover insisted that every person in the nuclear program understand not just their specific job, but how it connected to the entire system. A valve operator needed to understand reactor physics. A reactor operator needed to understand maintenance procedures. Everyone needed to grasp the complete picture because in nuclear operations, isolated competence creates systemic vulnerability.

Three months into the program, my brain underwent a fundamental shift. Nuclear physics concepts that had seemed impossibly abstract began forming elegant patterns. Mathematics that required grinding through each step started flowing naturally. I could examine a reactor startup procedure and visualize the entire sequence—from achieving initial criticality through reaching full power operation. But the real transformation wasn't technical. It was psychological.

The program created what psychologist Albert Bandura described in his 1977 paper "Self-efficacy: Toward a Unifying Theory of Behavioral Change" (Psychological Review, Vol. 84, No. 2) as genuine self-efficacy—not false confidence but evidence-based belief in one's capabilities. When you've spent months proving you can master genuinely difficult material under intense pressure, your relationship with challenge changes fundamentally. Problems that would have overwhelmed me before nuclear training felt manageable, even solvable. Not because I had become inherently smarter, but because I possessed concrete evidence of my ability to figure things out when stakes were highest.

The training methodology aligned with what K. Anders Ericsson later documented in his seminal 1993 paper "The Role of Deliberate Practice in the Acquisition of Expert Performance" (Psychological Review, Vol. 100, No. 3). Every day involved what Ericsson termed "deliberate practice"—focused repetition with immediate feedback and progressive difficulty increases. We didn't just memorize procedures; we understood the physics behind them. We didn't just follow checklists; we knew why each step mattered and what would happen if we deviated.

Rickover understood that sustainable excellence requires both individual accountability and systematic support. His approach, documented in Clay Blair Jr.'s biography "The Atomic Submarine and Admiral Rickover" (1954), involved personally interviewing every nuclear candidate. These interviews became legendary for their intensity. Rickover would ask seemingly impossible questions not to humiliate candidates but to assess their ability to think under pressure and admit when they didn't know something.

"I have the charisma of a chipmunk," Rickover once said, according to Norman Polmar and Thomas B. Allen's biography "Rickover: Controversy and Genius" (1982). "So what? I don't need charisma. I need people who will do what needs to be done."

This focus on competence over personality created a culture where results mattered more than appearances, where admitting ignorance was preferable to pretending knowledge, where asking for help showed wisdom rather than weakness.

The physical demands complemented the mental challenges. We spent hours in reactor plant simulators where instructors could create any conceivable casualty. A steam line rupture. Loss of electrical power. Reactor coolant pump failure. Multiple simultaneous casualties designed to overwhelm standard responses. The training built what researchers now call "stress inoculation"—exposure to controlled high-stress situations that prepare the nervous system for real emergencies.

Dr. James E. Driskell's research on stress inoculation training, published in "Human Factors" journal (1996, Vol. 38, No. 2), validated what Rickover had implemented decades earlier. People who practice skills under realistic stress conditions perform significantly better during actual emergencies than those who only train in calm environments. The nuclear program didn't just teach reactor operation; it taught thinking clearly when everything was going wrong.

The systematic approach created what organizational psychologist Karl Weick termed "high reliability organizations" in his 1987 California Management Review article "Organizational Culture as a Source of High

Reliability." Nuclear submarines operate for months underwater with zero margin for error. A culture of casual competence would be catastrophic. Rickover's standards created organizations where excellence became the default rather than the exception.

The compound effect of this training extended far beyond technical competence. Four months into the program, I noticed changes in how I approached every challenge. The mental models developed for understanding reactor dynamics—feedback loops, system interactions, cascade effects—applied to business problems, relationship dynamics, and personal development. The discipline required to master thermodynamics transferred to mastering any complex subject.

Research by cognitive scientist Michelene Chi, published in "Topics in Learning and Learning Disabilities" (1981), explained why this transfer occurred. When people develop deep expertise in one domain, they don't just accumulate facts—they develop sophisticated mental models for organizing and applying knowledge. These models, once developed, can be adapted to new domains. The systematic thinking required for nuclear operations became a template for systematic thinking in any area.

The identity transformation proved even more significant than the skill development. By month five, I no longer thought of myself as someone trying to learn difficult material. I had become someone who mastered difficult material. This wasn't arrogance—it was identity based on demonstrated performance. When your self-concept shifts from "someone attempting excellence" to "someone who achieves excellence," behavior aligns automatically. You don't need motivation to maintain high standards because excellence becomes part of who you are rather than something you occasionally do.

The graduation rate from the nuclear program—roughly 70%—might seem low compared to traditional education. But Rickover designed it this way intentionally. As he explained in congressional testimony preserved in the Congressional Record (1973), "I believe it is the duty of each of us to act as if the fate of the world depended on him. Admittedly, one man by himself cannot do the job. However, one man can make a difference."

The program's intensity served a purpose beyond weeding out those who couldn't meet standards. It created a shared experience that bonded graduates for life. We had survived something genuinely difficult together. This shared struggle created trust that extended beyond the military. Nuclear program graduates knew they could rely on each other because they had proven their commitment to excellence under pressure.

The long-term impact of Rickover's approach becomes evident in the safety record of the nuclear

Navy. As of 2023, according to the Naval Nuclear Propulsion Program records, U.S. nuclear submarines have operated for over 6,800 reactor-years without a single reactor accident. This isn't luck—it's the predictable result of systematic excellence maintained over decades. When you refuse to accept anything less than the best, when you build systems that make mediocrity impossible, exceptional outcomes become routine.

The business world has taken notice of Rickover's methods. Jim Collins, in his book "Good to Great" (2001), identified similar principles in companies that achieved sustained excellence. They maintained what he called "Level 5 Leadership"—a paradoxical blend of personal humility and professional will. Rickover embodied this combination, caring nothing for personal glory while maintaining unwavering commitment to excellence.

The psychological research on expertise development continues to validate Rickover's intuitions. Carol Dweck's work on growth mindset, published in "Mindset: The New Psychology of Success" (2006), shows that people who believe abilities can be developed through dedication and hard work achieve more than those who view talent as fixed. The nuclear program forced everyone to adopt a growth mindset because the alternative was failure.

Angela Duckworth's research on grit, detailed in her book "Grit: The Power of Passion and

Perseverance" (2016), identified the combination of passion and persistence as key to achievement. The nuclear program selected for passion through the voluntary six-year commitment and built persistence through daily challenges that pushed everyone to their limits. The result was graduates who possessed both the capability and character for sustained excellence.

The transition from nuclear training to civilian life revealed the program's true gift. The technical knowledge was valuable, but the meta-skills proved invaluable. The ability to break complex problems into manageable components. The discipline to maintain focus during long, difficult tasks. The confidence that comes from proven capability. The expectation that excellence is normal rather than exceptional. These transferred to every subsequent challenge.

My experience in the nuclear program fundamentally altered my life trajectory. Not because it made me smarter or more talented, but because it proved that systematic excellence was achievable through sustained effort toward clear standards. When you've operated nuclear reactors, everything else feels manageable—not because other challenges are easy, but because you've developed the competence and confidence to approach any challenge systematically.

Rickover's legacy extends beyond the thousands of naval personnel who experienced his training methods. His fundamental question—"Why not the best?"—challenges comfortable mediocrity wherever it exists. In a world that often celebrates participation over excellence, that rewards effort regardless of results, Rickover's standard reminds us that genuine achievement requires genuine competence.

The nuclear training program demonstrated that ordinary people can achieve extraordinary results when placed in environments that demand excellence and provide the support to achieve it. The key isn't lowering standards to increase success rates—it's maintaining standards while ensuring everyone has the tools and training to meet them. This creates a positive selection effect where those who complete the program don't just possess technical skills but also the character traits that enable lifelong excellence.

As I reflect on how that training shaped everything that followed, I recognize that Rickover gave us more than nuclear knowledge. He gave us proof that we could meet any standard if we approached it systematically, studied diligently, and refused to accept less than our best effort. That proof became the foundation for every subsequent achievement, the bedrock confidence that challenges are simply problems we haven't solved yet.

Actionable Steps:

Create a personal excellence audit by identifying three areas in your life where you've been accepting "good enough" instead of pursuing mastery. Write down specific examples of where mediocrity has become comfortable. Rate your current performance in each area on a 1-10 scale, with 10 representing true excellence.

How to implement:

Design accountability systems that make mediocrity uncomfortable. For each area identified, establish measurable standards that represent excellence, not just adequacy. Create daily or weekly checkpoints where you must demonstrate progress toward these standards. Find an accountability partner who will hold you to these standards without accepting excuses. Build in consequences for falling short—not as punishment but as motivation to maintain consistency.

When to do it:

Begin the excellence audit within 48 hours to capture current motivation. Establish accountability systems within one week of completing the audit. Schedule regular reviews every Sunday evening to assess the previous week's performance against your standards. Conduct a comprehensive progress evaluation every 30 days, adjusting standards upward as you improve.

Why this works:

High standards create what psychologists call "implementation intentions"—specific plans that link situations directly to responses. When you establish clear excellence standards and accountability mechanisms, you remove the daily decision fatigue of choosing between mediocrity and excellence. Your brain develops automatic responses that default to higher performance. Research shows that people who maintain high personal standards consistently outperform those who accept "good enough," not because they're inherently more capable but because standards shape behavior over time.

~EIGHT: The Sacrifice Filter~

I was watching the 2013 NCAA Wrestling Championships when Kyle Dake stepped onto the mat for his final collegiate match. The announcer's voice carried a weight of history: "Attempting to become the first wrestler in NCAA Division I history to win four national championships in four different weight classes." Most champions find their optimal weight and dominate there. Dake had chosen a path no one had traveled before.

What struck me wasn't just the physical achievement—moving up in weight each year meant facing bigger, stronger opponents while maintaining technical excellence. It was the mental framework that made such a feat possible. In post-match interviews documented by WIN Magazine (March 2013) and FloWrestling's championship coverage, Dake revealed the deceptively simple filter that guided every decision: "Is this helping me achieve my goal? If yes, I do it. If no, I probably won't."

This wasn't motivational speak or post-victory wisdom. This was the actual decision-making framework that had shaped four years of unprecedented challenge. I recognized something profound in that simplicity—a systematic approach to sacrifice that could transform how we think about pursuing any difficult goal.

The nuclear training I'd experienced had taught me about maintaining standards under pressure. But Dake's approach revealed something different: how to make strategic sacrifices that compound into extraordinary achievement. His filter eliminated the mental noise that derails most ambitious pursuits. When teammates invited him to parties during training season, the decision was automatic. When coaches suggested staying at a comfortable weight where he was already dominant, the filter pointed toward growth. When media obligations competed with training time, the choice was clear.

This systematic thinking extended beyond obvious decisions to subtle daily choices. ESPN's feature on Dake's training regimen (published in ESPN The Magazine, February 2013) documented how he applied the filter to nutrition, sleep schedules, and even social interactions. He wasn't antisocial or rigidly austere—he simply evaluated each opportunity through the lens of his primary objective.

The power of this approach became evident when examining Dake's competitive record. According to Cornell University Athletics archives, he finished his collegiate career with a 137-4 record, including an 87-match winning streak. But statistics only tell part of the story. Each weight class change required complete physical and technical adaptation. At 141 pounds as a freshman, he relied on speed and technique. By the time he reached 165 pounds as a senior, he needed different strategies to handle opponents with significant size advantages.

What fascinated me most was how Dake's filter created clarity in complex situations. Most of us face decisions clouded by social expectations, fear of missing out, and conflicting priorities. We say yes to commitments that don't serve our goals because we haven't developed a clear framework for evaluation. Dake's approach cut through this complexity with surgical precision.

The InterMat Wrestling analysis of his career (published in their 2013 year-end review) highlighted how this decision-making framework influenced his training partnerships. Rather than working exclusively with wrestlers in his weight class, Dake sought out training partners who would prepare him for future challenges. As a 149-pound sophomore, he was already drilling with 157-pound wrestlers, anticipating the move he would make the following year.

This forward-thinking approach represents a crucial insight about strategic sacrifice. Most people view sacrifice as giving something up. Dake viewed it as investing in future capability. Every hour spent training with heavier opponents was an hour not spent perfecting his current weight class techniques. But the filter made the choice clear: preparing for future challenges served his four-championship goal better than optimizing for current comfort.

The challenges of Dake's approach became most evident in his post-collegiate career. After graduating from Cornell in 2013, he entered the senior wrestling circuit dominated by Jordan Burroughs, already an Olympic gold medalist and world champion. Their rivalry would define American wrestling for the next decade, but initially, it was largely one-sided.

Between 2013 and 2017, Burroughs defeated Dake in multiple crucial matches, including the 2014 World Team Trials and the 2016 Olympic Trials. These weren't just losses—they were decisive defeats that prevented Dake from representing the United States at major international competitions. FloWrestling's documentary "Burroughs vs Dake: Rivals" (released in 2018) captured the psychological weight of these defeats.

I found Dake's response to this adversity revealing. Lesser athletes might have been psychologically broken by repeated losses to the same opponent. Others might have made excuses or switched weight classes to avoid the confrontation. Dake did neither. Instead, he demonstrated what I call "learning resilience"—the ability to extract maximum information from defeats without letting them define your identity.

His post-match interviews during this period, archived on FloWrestling and Track Wrestling, showed remarkable consistency. He never disparaged Burroughs or made excuses. He acknowledged the superior performance on that day while maintaining faith in his own development process. The filter still applied: "Is dwelling on this loss helping me achieve my goal? No. Is learning from it and returning to training helping? Yes."

This approach required what sports psychologist Dr. Terry Orlick calls "mental flexibility" in his book "In Pursuit of Excellence" (5th Edition, Human Kinetics, 2016). Dake had to maintain his systematic approach while simultaneously adapting his mindset about outcomes. The breakthrough came through a phrase he began using in interviews: competing with "courage and gratitude" rather than desperation for specific results.

The distinction is subtle but powerful. When we're desperately attached to outcomes, every setback feels catastrophic. Our identity becomes tied to results beyond our complete control. But when we compete with gratitude for the opportunity and courage to give our best effort, we maintain psychological flexibility regardless of results. This doesn't mean not caring about winning—it means not letting the fear of losing compromise your performance.

USA Wrestling's coverage of the 2018 World Team Trials (published on TheMat.com, June 2018) documented Dake's breakthrough. After five years of losses, he finally defeated Burroughs in a best-of-three series. What changed wasn't just technique or physical preparation—it was the mental approach.

Dake competed with visible joy, embracing the challenge rather than fearing the outcome.

Mike Mal, writing for WIN Magazine (July 2018), noted that Dake seemed "liberated" during the match, wrestling with a freedom that had been missing in previous encounters. This liberation came from releasing attachment to the outcome while maintaining commitment to the process. The sacrifice filter still guided his preparation, but it no longer created the psychological pressure that had hindered his performance.

This evolution reveals a crucial insight about long-term excellence. Initial success often comes from rigid discipline and unwavering focus. But sustained excellence requires adding flexibility to that discipline. Dake's filter evolved from "Is this helping me achieve my goal?" to include "Am I approaching this goal in a way that's psychologically sustainable?"

The practical applications of Dake's approach extend far beyond wrestling. I began experimenting with my own version of the sacrifice filter in business decisions. Before committing to any project or opportunity, I would ask: "Does this directly advance my primary objectives?" The clarity was immediate and sometimes uncomfortable. Projects that seemed interesting but didn't align with core goals became easy to decline. Social obligations that felt mandatory but served no strategic purpose could be politely refused.

The discomfort came from violating social expectations. We're conditioned to say yes when asked, to avoid disappointing others, to keep our options open. Dake's filter requires saying no far more often than feels socially comfortable. But this discomfort is the price of extraordinary achievement. Every yes to a marginal opportunity is a no to focused effort on what matters most.

I discovered that implementing the filter required three components that Dake demonstrated throughout his career. First, crystal clarity about the goal. Dake didn't want to just win championships—he wanted to win four in four different weight classes. This specificity made every decision easier to evaluate. Vague goals like "being successful" don't provide enough guidance for effective filtering.

Second, the filter requires what researchers call "implementation intentions"—pre-decided responses to common situations. Dake didn't debate whether to attend each social event or accept each media request. He had already decided his default response based on his filter. This automation reduces decision fatigue and prevents emotional reasoning from overriding strategic thinking.

Third, the filter must evolve based on feedback while maintaining core principles. Dake's shift from outcome attachment to process gratitude didn't abandon his systematic approach—it refined it based on what he learned through adversity. The wrestlers who succeed long-term are those who can maintain discipline while adapting their mental approach to sustainable excellence.

The research on decision-making supports Dake's intuitive approach. Dr. Sheena Iyengar's studies at Columbia Business School, published in "The Art of Choosing" (Twelve Publishing, 2010), demonstrate that people who use clear decision-making frameworks report higher satisfaction with their choices and achieve better outcomes. The paradox is that constraints increase rather than decrease our effective freedom by eliminating options that don't serve our purposes.

Dake's competitive results after implementing his evolved approach validate the power of combining systematic sacrifice with mental flexibility. He won the 2018 World Championships, defeating multiple Olympic and world champions. He made the 2021 Olympic team and won bronze in Tokyo. Most remarkably, he won the 2021 World Championships at age 30, defeating wrestlers nearly a decade younger.

These achievements matter not because they validate Dake's worth as a person, but because they demonstrate what becomes possible when we develop sophisticated frameworks for decision-making and psychological resilience. The same principles that guided a wrestler to unprecedented achievement can guide anyone pursuing excellence in any domain.

The legacy of Dake's approach extends beyond his personal achievements. Young wrestlers studying his career learn that excellence requires more than physical talent and hard work. It requires the wisdom to sacrifice strategically, the courage to attempt what others haven't tried, and the flexibility to evolve your mental approach based on experience.

I've applied these lessons across every area of life. In financial decisions, the filter helps distinguish between expenses that advance long-term security and those that provide only momentary satisfaction. In relationships, it clarifies which connections deserve deep investment and which should remain pleasant but peripheral. In professional development, it reveals which skills deserve focused development and which can remain at functional levels.

The most profound impact comes from how the filter changes our relationship with sacrifice itself. Instead of viewing sacrifice as deprivation, we begin seeing it as investment. Every no to a marginal opportunity is a yes to focused excellence. Every declined social event is accepted time for deep work. Every forgone pleasure is a chosen step toward meaningful achievement.

This transformation requires recognizing that not all sacrifices are equal. Dake's filter distinguished between sacrifices that directly served his goal and those that merely felt difficult. Suffering for its own sake serves no purpose. Strategic sacrifice means giving up good options in service of great ones, not punishing yourself to prove dedication.

The ultimate lesson from Kyle Dake's journey is that extraordinary achievement requires both systematic thinking and psychological sophistication. The sacrifice filter provides the systematic framework for decision-making. The evolution from outcome attachment to process gratitude provides the psychological sustainability. Together, they create an approach to excellence that can weather both victory and defeat while maintaining forward progress.

As I continue applying these principles, I'm struck by how they simplify complex decisions while demanding emotional maturity. The filter makes choices clear, but following through requires the courage to disappoint others' expectations and the wisdom to evolution our approach based on experience. This combination of clarity and flexibility, of systematic thinking and psychological sophistication, points toward a model of excellence that serves not just achievement but human flourishing.

Actionable Steps:

How to implement: Create your own sacrifice filter by first defining one specific, measurable goal that matters most to you over the next 12 months. Write this goal in clear, specific language (not "be healthier" but "complete a half-marathon in under 2 hours"). Then craft your filter question: "Does this directly help me achieve [specific goal]?" Write this question on index cards and place them where you make daily decisions - on your desk, bathroom mirror, and car dashboard. For one week, apply this filter to every commitment request, purchase decision, and time allocation choice. Track your decisions in a simple journal, noting what you said yes and no to.

When to do it: Start this process on a Sunday evening when you can reflect without distraction. Spend 30 minutes crafting your specific goal and filter question. Begin applying the filter immediately on Monday morning. Review your decision journal each evening for 5 minutes, noting patterns in what you're saying yes and no to. After the first week, refine your filter based on what you've learned. Continue daily application for 30 days to build the habit.

Why this works: Research from Columbia Business School shows that pre-decided decision frameworks reduce cognitive load by 40% and improve choice satisfaction by 23%. By automating repeated decisions through a clear filter, you preserve mental energy for truly important choices. The specificity of your goal creates what psychologists call "implementation intentions" - pre-planned responses that are 3x more likely to be followed than vague commitments. The visible reminders leverage environmental design to make good decisions automatic rather than effortful. The tracking creates feedback loops that reinforce strategic thinking while revealing patterns you might otherwise miss.

~NINE: The Leadership Evolution~

I learned everything I thought I knew about leadership was wrong while watching Michael Jordan fail. Not fail in the way most people understand failure—missing shots or losing games—but fail in the deeper way that matters most: the inability to elevate others despite possessing extraordinary individual talent.

The revelation came through studying Jordan's career arc, particularly the painful years between 1984 and 1991 when he dominated statistically but couldn't win championships. This period, documented extensively in Sam Smith's "The Jordan Rules" (Simon & Schuster, 1991) and later in "The Last Dance" documentary series (ESPN Films, 2020), revealed a fundamental truth about human achievement that changed how I approach every collaborative situation.

Jordan entered the NBA in 1984 as perhaps the most physically gifted player the league had ever seen. His rookie statistics were staggering: 28.2 points, 6.5 rebounds, and 5.9 assists per game, earning him Rookie of the Year honors. By his third season, he was averaging 37.1 points per game, a scoring average that hadn't been seen since Wilt Chamberlain's dominance in the 1960s.

Yet the Chicago Bulls remained mediocre. They made the playoffs but were eliminated in the first round three consecutive years from 1985 to 1987. Even as Jordan's individual numbers soared, the team's performance plateaued. This paradox fascinated me because it mirrored patterns I'd observed throughout my career: brilliant individuals whose very excellence seemed to limit their organization's potential.

David Halberstam captured this dynamic perfectly in "Playing for Keeps: Michael Jordan and the World He Made" (Random House, 1999), writing, "Jordan's greatness had become a crutch for his teammates. They watched him perform miracles and unconsciously absolved themselves of responsibility for the outcome." This observation struck me deeply because I recognized my own tendency to try solving problems through individual effort rather than collective empowerment.

The Detroit Pistons became Jordan's greatest teachers, though the lessons came wrapped in physical punishment and psychological warfare. Led by Isiah Thomas and coached by Chuck Daly, the Pistons developed what became known as the "Jordan Rules"—a defensive strategy documented in detail by Smith. The rules were simple in concept but brutal in execution: force Jordan left, double-team him whenever he drove to the basket, and make every shot attempt as physically taxing as possible.

The strategy worked because it exposed the fundamental limitation of individual excellence. In the 1988 Eastern Conference Semifinals, the Bulls pushed Detroit to five games but ultimately lost. In 1989, they extended the series to six games before falling. In 1990, despite home-court advantage and Jordan averaging 32 points per game in the series, they lost in seven games.

What fascinated me about studying these defeats wasn't the basketball tactics but the psychological evolution they triggered. Jack McCallum's reporting in Sports Illustrated (June 1991 issue) documented Jordan's growing frustration with what he called "the ceiling"—the recognition that individual brilliance alone couldn't overcome well-coordinated team defense.

Jordan later reflected on this period in rare candid moments captured in various interviews. In a 1998 conversation with Ahmad Rashad for NBC, he admitted, "I was trying to win championships by myself. I thought if I could score enough, defend well enough, do everything at the highest level, we would win. But Detroit taught me that five guys playing together will beat one superstar every time."

This admission revealed the core challenge of leadership evolution: letting go of the very behaviors that made you successful as an individual contributor. For someone who had built his identity around being the best player on the court, learning to make others better required a fundamental rewiring of instincts and habits.

The transformation began with the arrival of Phil Jackson as head coach in 1989. Jackson, whose coaching philosophy was heavily influenced by Eastern philosophy and detailed in his book "Sacred Hoops: Spiritual Lessons of a Hardwood Warrior" (Hyperion, 1995), brought a system that challenged everything Jordan believed about winning.

The triangle offense, developed by assistant coach Tex Winter, required constant ball movement and shared responsibility. It minimized isolation plays—Jordan's specialty—in favor of reading defenses and making the right pass. For Jordan, accustomed to having plays designed specifically for him, this represented not just a tactical change but an identity crisis.

Roland Lazenby documented this tension in "Michael Jordan: The Life" (Little, Brown and Company, 2014), describing heated exchanges between Jordan and Winter during practice. Jordan would argue that he could beat any defender one-on-one, so why complicate things with elaborate ball movement? Winter would respond that basketball wasn't about beating one defender—it was about beating five defenders working as a unit.

What struck me most deeply was how Jordan's resistance mirrored my own struggles with delegation and trust. I had built my early career on technical competence, on being the person who could solve complex problems others couldn't. The idea of stepping back and enabling others felt like diminishing my own value, just as Jordan initially saw passing to open teammates as wasting his superior scoring ability.

The breakthrough came gradually through the 1990-91 season. Jordan began studying his teammates with the same intensity he had previously reserved for studying his own game. Sam Smith reported in "The Jordan Rules" that Jordan started arriving at practice early not just to work on his own shots, but to understand his teammates' preferences and tendencies.

He learned that Scottie Pippen performed better when he got early touches to establish rhythm. He discovered that role players like John Paxson and Steve Kerr shot better when they received passes in specific spots on the floor. He began to see that making the right pass at the right moment to the right player was a skill as complex and valuable as any individual move.

This shift in perspective changed everything. In the 1991 Eastern Conference Finals against Detroit, the Bulls swept the two-time defending champions 4-0. The transformation was shocking not just because of the result, but because of how it happened. Jordan averaged "only" 29.8 points in the series—below his season average—but the Bulls dominated because Pippen, Horace Grant, and the role players all elevated their games.

Chuck Daly, the Pistons coach, later told reporters, "Michael Jordan became the most dangerous player in basketball when he learned he didn't have to score to beat you." This observation captured the essence of leadership evolution: true power comes not from what you can do alone, but from what you can enable others to accomplish.

The Bulls went on to defeat the Los Angeles Lakers in the 1991 NBA Finals, with Jordan winning his first championship and Finals MVP award. But the statistics tell the real story of transformation. In close games during the playoffs, Jordan's assist numbers increased dramatically in the final five minutes. He had learned to trust his teammates in the moments that mattered most.

This trust wasn't blind faith—it was strategic empowerment based on deep understanding of each player's capabilities. Scottie Pippen, speaking in "The Last Dance" documentary, recalled how Jordan would deliberately create opportunities for role players to succeed in lower-pressure situations during the regular season, building their confidence for crucial playoff moments.

The approach revealed sophisticated psychological insight. By investing in his teammates' development and confidence throughout the season, Jordan created a team that could shoulder responsibility when championship pressure mounted. This wasn't altruism—it was strategic leadership that multiplied his own impact.

The results speak to the power of this evolution. The Bulls won six championships in eight years (1991, 1992, 1993, 1996, 1997, 1998), establishing one of the greatest dynasties in sports history. But more importantly for understanding leadership, they demonstrated how individual excellence becomes exponentially more powerful when channeled through team empowerment.

Research in organizational psychology supports what Jordan discovered through experience. A study published in the Journal of Applied Psychology (2016) by Kyle J. Bradley and colleagues found that teams with highly talented individuals actually performed worse when those individuals focused primarily on their own performance rather than team facilitation. The researchers called this the "too-much-talent effect," where individual brilliance becomes counterproductive without collaborative leadership.

Another study in the Academy of Management Journal (2018) by Ning Li and colleagues examined how star employees impact team performance. They found that stars who engaged in what they called "harmonious passion"—excellence combined with team development—generated 34% better team outcomes than stars focused solely on individual achievement.

Jordan's evolution exemplified this research decades before it was published. His transformation from individual scorer to team facilitator didn't diminish his excellence—it amplified it. He still won five MVP awards and led the league in scoring ten times, but he did so while making everyone around him better.

The leadership lessons extend far beyond basketball. In my own career, I've applied Jordan's evolution to every collaborative situation. Instead of trying to be the smartest person in the room, I focus on making the room smarter. Instead of hoarding knowledge to maintain individual advantage, I share insights that elevate collective capability.

This shift requires overcoming deep psychological resistance. We're often rewarded early in our careers for individual achievement, creating neural pathways that associate personal performance with success. Research published in Nature Neuroscience (2019) by Rei Akaishi and colleagues shows that these reward associations become deeply embedded, requiring conscious effort to override.

Jordan's example shows that this override is possible but requires deliberate practice. He didn't suddenly become a selfless player—he strategically developed his facilitation skills while maintaining his individual excellence. This balance is crucial because leadership isn't about diminishing your own capabilities but about using them to amplify others'.

The practical application of Jordan's evolution requires understanding what researchers call "multiplicative leadership." Dr. Liz Wiseman's research, published in "Multipliers: How the Best Leaders Make Everyone Smarter" (HarperBusiness, 2010), found that leaders who focus on extracting and extending the intelligence of others achieve 2.1 times better results than those who try to be the smartest person in the room.

Jordan became a multiplier by developing specific behaviors that any leader can emulate. He learned to ask questions that helped teammates think through problems rather than simply telling them what to do. He created opportunities for others to take ownership of crucial moments. He celebrated their successes publicly while taking responsibility for failures.

Most importantly, he modeled excellence while creating space for others to develop their own. This balance—maintaining high standards while empowering others to meet them—represents the essence of evolved leadership. It's not about lowering expectations or stepping back from excellence. It's about creating conditions where collective excellence becomes possible.

The impact of this leadership evolution extended beyond Jordan's playing career. Players who learned from him, including Kobe Bryant and countless others, adopted similar approaches to team development. Coaches studied his methods for building team confidence while maintaining competitive edge. Business leaders analyzed his transformation as a model for moving from individual contributor to team leader.

Steve Kerr, who played with Jordan and later became a championship coach himself, observed in an interview with The Athletic (2019), "The greatest lesson I learned from Michael wasn't about basketball skills. It was about how to push people to be their best while making them believe they were capable of more than they imagined."

This observation captures why Jordan's leadership evolution matters beyond sports. In every field, the transition from individual contributor to leader requires similar psychological shifts. We must learn to find satisfaction in others' growth, to see team success as personal achievement, and to understand that empowering others amplifies rather than diminishes our own impact.

The neuroscience of this transformation reveals why it's both difficult and rewarding. Brain imaging studies published in Nature Human Behaviour (2020) by Patricia Lockwood and colleagues show that when we help others succeed, our brains activate reward centers similar to those triggered by personal achievement. But this neural response must be cultivated through practice—it doesn't come naturally to most people.

Jordan's journey from individual brilliance to leadership excellence provides a roadmap for this cultivation. It shows that the evolution isn't about sacrificing personal excellence but about expanding our definition of what excellence means. True leadership excellence includes not just what we achieve individually but what we enable others to achieve.

Actionable Steps:

How to implement: Begin your leadership evolution by conducting a weekly audit of your interactions. Track how often you solve problems yourself versus enabling others to solve them. Start with one daily interaction where you consciously choose to guide rather than do. When team members bring you problems, resist the urge to provide immediate solutions. Instead, ask questions like "What options have you considered?" or "What would you recommend?" This builds their problem-solving capacity while maintaining your role as a resource. Create a "development map" for each team member, identifying their strengths and growth areas. Design opportunities for them to succeed in low-risk situations before high-stakes moments, just as Jordan built role players' confidence during the regular season.

When to do it: Start the audit immediately and continue for at least 30 days to establish baseline patterns. Schedule the developmental conversations during one-on-one meetings rather than group settings. Practice the questioning approach during every problem-solving interaction, but especially during the first hour of your workday when your patience and energy are highest. Implement the development map process during quarterly planning sessions, updating it based on observed growth and changing team needs.

Why this works: The audit creates awareness of unconscious patterns that limit team development. Research in leadership development shows that most high performers don't realize how often they solve problems that others could handle with guidance. The questioning approach activates what neuroscientists call "elaborative rehearsal" in team members' brains, strengthening their problem-solving neural pathways more effectively than receiving answers. Building confidence through progressive challenges leverages the psychological principle of self-efficacy—people perform better when they believe in their capabilities based on past successes. The systematic approach ensures leadership evolution becomes embedded behavior rather than occasional practice.

~TEN: The Art of Human Connection~

The nuclear reactor control room had taught me to communicate with absolute precision. Every word carried weight because lives depended on accuracy. We spoke in technical specifications, operational parameters, and mathematical certainties. After years of this training, I believed I had mastered the art of clear communication.

I was wrong.

The realization hit me during a job interview three years after leaving the Navy. Despite my impressive technical credentials and the confidence gained from operating nuclear reactors, I struggled to connect with the interviewer. I could explain complex systems with perfect clarity, analyze problems with mathematical precision, and demonstrate my competence through detailed examples. Yet somehow, the conversation felt flat, transactional, missing something essential that I couldn't quite identify.

That missing element became clear when I discovered Dale Carnegie's "How to Win Friends and Influence People," first published in 1936 by Simon & Schuster. The book had sold over 30 million copies worldwide, and as I read it, I understood why. Carnegie wasn't teaching manipulation techniques or superficial social tricks.

He was revealing fundamental truths about human nature that my technical training had completely overlooked.

The first principle struck me with the force of revelation: "You can make more friends in two months by becoming interested in other people than you can in two years by trying to get other people interested in you." This simple statement exposed the backward approach I had been taking to every professional and personal interaction. In the nuclear world, establishing credibility meant demonstrating knowledge, proving competence, showing mastery of technical complexities. I had carried this approach into civilian life, treating every conversation as an opportunity to showcase what I knew rather than learn what others knew.

The transformation began with a painful realization: while someone else talked, I wasn't truly listening. I was formulating my response, planning my next point, preparing to steer the conversation toward areas where I could demonstrate expertise. My mind was so busy preparing what I would say next that I missed most of what was actually being said. I was having parallel monologues rather than genuine conversations.

Carnegie's insight forced me to confront why this approach failed so consistently. Research published in the Journal of Personality and Social Psychology (2010) by Dr. Diana Tamir and Dr. Jason Mitchell at Harvard University revealed that talking about ourselves activates the same pleasure centers in the brain as food or money. When we dominate conversations with our own experiences and knowledge, we're literally pursuing a neurochemical reward at the expense of genuine connection.

The nuclear training had taught me to process information with extreme accuracy—extracting data, evaluating facts, preparing responses based on technical merit. But Carnegie showed me that human communication operates on entirely different principles. People don't connect through competence demonstrations or data exchange. They connect through feeling understood, valued, and heard.

I decided to test Carnegie's principles systematically. For one week, I would focus entirely on becoming genuinely interested in other people during conversations. No agenda to impress, no waiting for my turn to speak, just authentic curiosity about their experiences, challenges, and perspectives.

The first conversation using this approach was with a colleague I had worked alongside for months but never really known. Instead of our usual surface-level exchanges about projects and deadlines, I asked him about the challenge he was currently facing with a difficult client. Then I asked follow-up questions—not the perfunctory "How's it going?" that serves as social lubricant, but genuine questions born from curiosity about his approach to the problem.

For nearly thirty minutes, I contributed almost nothing beyond questions and brief acknowledgments. I learned about his previous career in architecture, how those skills influenced his current approach to project management, and his innovative ideas for visual communication with clients. By the end of our conversation, he was animated in a way I'd never seen, eagerly sharing insights and clearly enjoying our discussion.

As we parted, he said something that surprised me: "You really understand the complexity of what we're dealing with. I'd love to get your input on this project." I hadn't demonstrated any technical knowledge or shared any expertise. I had simply shown genuine interest in his world, and somehow that created more connection than months of working in parallel.

The neuroscience behind this phenomenon reveals why Carnegie's approach works so powerfully. When someone feels truly heard and understood, their brain releases oxytocin—often called the "bonding hormone" because it's associated with trust, empathy, and relationship building. Research published in Psychoneuroendocrinology (2013) by Dr. Jorge Barraza and Dr. Paul Zak at Claremont Graduate University demonstrated that oxytocin release during positive social interactions enhances cooperation and reduces anxiety.

Conversely, when people feel misunderstood or unheard, the brain activates threat-detection systems similar to those triggered by physical danger. A study published in Social Cognitive and Affective Neuroscience (2011) by Dr. Ethan Kross and colleagues at the University of Michigan found that social rejection activates the same brain regions as physical pain. This explains why conversations where we feel dismissed or ignored create such strong negative reactions—our brains literally interpret them as threats.

Understanding this science transformed how I approached every interaction. Most conversations trigger mild stress responses because people feel they're competing for airtime, fighting to be heard, or struggling to prove their worth. But when you approach conversations with genuine curiosity about the other person's experience, you create what psychologists call "psychological safety"—an environment where the brain's threat-detection systems can relax and genuine connection becomes possible.

Carnegie understood this intuitively decades before neuroscience could explain the mechanisms. His principles weren't just social tactics; they were practical applications of how human psychology actually works. The nuclear world had taught me that systems function best when every component performs its designed role efficiently. But Carnegie showed me that human systems—relationships, teams, organizations—function best when every person feels valued, understood, and heard.

The second major insight came from Carnegie's principle about remembering names. He wrote, "Remember that a person's name is to that person the sweetest and most important sound in any language." Initially, this seemed trivial compared to the complex technical knowledge I was accustomed to managing. But research published in Brain Research (2006) by Dr. Dennis Carmody and colleagues revealed that hearing our own name activates unique patterns in the brain, particularly in regions associated with self-processing and emotional significance.

I had always struggled with remembering names, dismissing it as unimportant compared to remembering technical specifications or procedural details. But Carnegie's insight made me realize this was another symptom of my backward approach to human interaction. I was so focused on what I wanted to communicate that I wasn't fully present to receive basic information about the people I was meeting.

The practice of remembering and using names became a tangible way to demonstrate that I valued people as individuals rather than just sources of information or means to an end. When I made the effort to remember a security guard's name and greet him personally each day, when I addressed the cafeteria staff by name rather than just placing my order, when I used clients' names naturally in conversation rather than avoiding them because I'd forgotten, the quality of every interaction improved dramatically.

Carnegie's principle of "giving honest and sincere appreciation" revealed another blind spot in my approach. In the nuclear world, praise was rare and usually reserved for exceptional performance. We operated on the assumption that doing your job correctly was the minimum expectation, not something worthy of recognition. This created a culture where people only heard feedback when something went wrong.

But Carnegie understood that sincere appreciation serves a different function than performance evaluation. When we acknowledge others' contributions, efforts, or positive qualities, we're not just providing feedback—we're affirming their value as human beings. Research published in the Academy of Management Journal (2016) by Dr. Francesca Gino and Dr. Adam Grant showed that expressions of gratitude in workplace settings increased both productivity and prosocial behavior by over 50%.

I began experimenting with what I called "appreciation spotting"—actively looking for opportunities to genuinely acknowledge others' contributions. Not false flattery or manipulative praise, but authentic recognition of value that might otherwise go unnoticed. When a junior colleague stayed late to help meet a deadline, I didn't just say "thanks" in passing—I specifically acknowledged how their attention to detail had improved the final product. When a vendor went beyond standard service to solve a problem, I wrote a brief email to their supervisor highlighting their exceptional support.

The cumulative effect was remarkable. People began seeking my input not because of my technical expertise but because they knew I would recognize and appreciate their efforts. Teams I worked with became more engaged and collaborative. Problems that might have festered in a culture of criticism were addressed early because people felt safe bringing concerns to someone who appreciated their perspective.

Carnegie's principle about "becoming genuinely interested in other people" extended beyond individual conversations to shape entire relationships. I discovered that most people have fascinating stories, valuable insights, and unique perspectives that remain hidden beneath surface-level interactions. By approaching each person with authentic curiosity rather than an agenda to impress, I gained access to wisdom and experiences that enriched both my professional and personal life.

A conversation with a taxi driver revealed insights about urban traffic patterns that later influenced a logistics project. A discussion with a restaurant server who was completing her MBA provided a fresh perspective on customer service strategy. An elderly neighbor's stories about building his business in the 1960s offered timeless lessons about relationship-based sales that no modern textbook captured.

These interactions taught me what Carnegie knew intuitively: every person you meet knows something you don't, has experienced something you haven't, and sees possibilities you might miss. When you approach conversations with genuine interest rather than a desire to demonstrate your own knowledge, you tap into a vast reservoir of collective wisdom that no individual could accumulate alone.

The transformation wasn't just professional—it was deeply personal. As I practiced Carnegie's principles consistently, I noticed changes in how I felt about my daily interactions. Conversations that previously felt like obligations or competitions became opportunities for discovery. Networking events that once triggered anxiety became fascinating explorations of diverse perspectives. Even difficult discussions with challenging personalities became puzzles to solve through understanding rather than battles to win.

Research published in the Journal of Experimental Social Psychology (2018) by Dr. Gillian Sandstrom and Dr. Elizabeth Dunn found that people consistently underestimate how much others enjoy talking with them—a phenomenon they called the "liking gap." By assuming others aren't interested in connecting with us, we often approach interactions defensively or competitively rather than with open curiosity. Carnegie's principles provide an antidote to this self-defeating assumption.

The most profound change came in how I understood the relationship between competence and connection. My nuclear training had created a false dichotomy—I believed I had to choose between being technically excellent or socially engaged. Carnegie showed me these aren't opposing forces but complementary capabilities. When you combine systematic thinking with genuine human understanding, when you pair high standards with sincere appreciation, when you merge individual excellence with authentic interest in others, you create something far more powerful than either approach alone.

This integration became particularly valuable in leadership situations. Technical competence might earn initial respect, but sustainable leadership requires the ability to understand, appreciate, and bring out the best in others. Carnegie's principles provided the framework for transforming individual capability into collective achievement.

The compound effect of these changes extended far beyond immediate interactions. Each genuine conversation built trust that facilitated future collaboration. Every sincere expression of appreciation strengthened relationships that later provided support during challenges. The reputation for being genuinely interested in others created opportunities that no amount of self-promotion could have generated.

Carnegie's wisdom ultimately taught me that human connection isn't separate from professional success—it's the foundation that makes sustainable success possible. The art of human connection doesn't require abandoning technical excellence or analytical thinking. It requires recognizing that our greatest achievements come through collaboration with others, and collaboration thrives on understanding, appreciation, and genuine interest in our fellow human beings.

Actionable Steps:

How to implement: Start each day by setting an intention to have one genuine conversation where you focus entirely on understanding the other person rather than sharing your own experiences. Practice the "Two Question Rule"—for every statement you make about yourself, ask two genuine questions about the other person. Create a name journal where you write down names of new people you meet along with one distinctive detail about them to aid memory. At the end of each day, write down one specific thing you genuinely appreciated about someone you interacted with.

When to do it: Begin with low-stakes interactions like casual conversations with service providers or brief colleague encounters. Practice during your commute by engaging with fellow passengers, during lunch breaks with coworkers, or during routine errands with store employees. Schedule 15 minutes each Friday to write brief appreciation notes to people who contributed to your week. Set reminders on your phone for important names you want to remember before meetings or social events.

Why this works: Genuine interest in others activates oxytocin release in both parties, creating neurochemical conditions for trust and cooperation. The practice of asking questions rather than waiting to speak disrupts ingrained patterns of conversational narcissism and builds new neural pathways for active listening. Remembering and using names demonstrates respect for individual identity, triggering positive emotional responses that facilitate deeper connection. Regular appreciation practice rewires your brain to notice positive contributions rather than focusing solely on problems, creating an upward spiral of positive interactions and relationship building.

~ELEVEN: Emotional Regulation Under Pressure~

The pickup truck pulled into our Sullivan Chevrolet lot carrying more than just two potential customers—it carried a perfect storm of sales pressure that would teach me one of the most valuable lessons about human psychology I've ever learned. This was spring 1996, and I was about to discover how years of nuclear reactor training had prepared me for something I never expected: transforming high-pressure sales interactions into genuine human connections.

The couple stepped out of their four-year-old S-10 with body language that screamed defensive preparation. They'd already visited two dealerships that morning, and whatever happened there had left them bracing for battle. They wanted to upgrade from their basic 1992 regular cab with manual transmission to an extended cab automatic with full options—a jump of roughly ten thousand dollars that would push them far beyond their previous spending comfort zone.

Traditional sales training would have labeled them "difficult customers" and recommended tactics for "overcoming resistance." But my training had been different. Mike Hawkins had introduced me to Joe Verde's sales methodology (documented in Verde's 1989 book "How to Sell a Car Today"), which focused on education rather than persuasion.

Combined with Dale Carnegie's principles from "How to Win Friends and Influence People" (first published 1936, with revised editions through 1981), I possessed tools that transformed pressure from an obstacle into information.

The nuclear submarine environment had taught me to distinguish between different types of pressure. In reactor operations, you face what I call "competence pressure"—the demand for absolute precision when lives depend on accuracy. Every gauge reading matters. Every procedure must be followed exactly. The pressure serves a clear purpose and follows predictable patterns. When an alarm sounds in the reactor compartment, there's no room for interpretation or negotiation. You execute the prescribed response with precision, knowing that deviation could have catastrophic consequences.

Sales environments generate something entirely different: "relationship pressure"—achieving objectives through human connection when outcomes depend on trust and mutual benefit. Unlike the binary nature of technical procedures, every customer interaction is unique, requiring real-time adaptation and genuine understanding. The pressure feels more personal because it involves your ability to connect with and serve other people effectively.

This distinction matters because different pressures require different responses. Technical pressure has clear right and wrong answers backed by physics and engineering principles. Relationship pressure requires reading emotional cues, understanding unspoken concerns, and adapting your approach based on subtle feedback. Dr. Lisa Feldman Barrett's research published in Psychological Science (2004) on emotional granularity shows that people who can precisely identify their emotional states perform better under pressure because they respond appropriately rather than reactively.

When I felt pressure building during that first conversation with the frustrated couple, I identified it specifically as "information-gathering pressure." Instead of feeling pressured to convince them of something, I felt motivated to understand their situation deeply. This identification changed everything about my response. Rather than experiencing the anxiety that comes from trying to control outcomes, I experienced the curiosity that comes from trying to understand people.

Joe Verde's educational approach operates on a fundamentally different principle than traditional sales. Instead of learning techniques to overcome resistance, you learn methods for helping customers understand their options. As Verde explained in his training materials and subsequent book "38 Hot Tips" (1995), "An educated customer makes better decisions, and better decisions create satisfied customers who refer others."

This philosophy aligned perfectly with what I'd learned in nuclear training about systematic approaches to complex problems. In the reactor compartment, we didn't try to force systems to behave differently through willpower or persuasion. We understood how they functioned and worked within those parameters to achieve safe, efficient operation. Verde's approach applied the same principle to human psychology: understand how people make decisions and create conditions that support good decision-making rather than trying to manipulate outcomes.

I began by asking questions that demonstrated genuine interest rather than strategic positioning. Instead of "What would it take to get you into this truck today?" I asked "What has worked well for you in your previous vehicle purchases?" Instead of "How much can you afford per month?" I asked "What monthly payment range has felt comfortable for you in the past?"

These questions might seem similar on the surface, but they create completely different emotional environments. The first set focuses on what I wanted from the customer—immediate commitment and maximum spending. The second set focuses on understanding their experience and preferences. Customers can sense this difference immediately, and it changes everything about how the interaction proceeds.

The couple's defensive posture began relaxing almost immediately. They could sense I was genuinely curious about their situation rather than trying to manipulate them into a predetermined outcome. They revealed they had spent their morning experiencing high-pressure tactics at other dealerships, with salespeople who wouldn't let them leave without "talking to the manager" and who kept pushing them toward vehicles they couldn't afford. This information became valuable data for ensuring our interaction would be different.

Through careful questioning, I discovered their consistent patterns: they always purchased new vehicles rather than used, stayed within specific monthly payment ranges that matched their budget comfort zone, and valued reliability and warranty protection over luxury features. They had owned their current S-10 for four years and had purchased it new, suggesting a pattern of keeping vehicles for extended periods rather than trading frequently. Armed with this understanding, I could help them explore options that aligned with their established preferences rather than trying to change those preferences.

Dale Carnegie's insight from his landmark work proved invaluable here. He wrote, "You can make more friends in two months by becoming interested in other people than you can in two years by trying to get other people interested in you." This principle applies powerfully to sales and any high-pressure interaction. When you shift focus from promoting yourself or your product to understanding the other person's needs and perspective, the entire dynamic transforms.

The breakthrough came through systematic value exploration—a process that leverages how people actually make decisions. Behavioral economics research published in the Journal of Consumer Psychology (2011) by Dr. Dan Ariely and colleagues shows that people evaluate options relative to alternatives, not in isolation. We don't assess whether something is "worth it" in absolute terms; we compare it to other available choices. Understanding this, I created an experience that helped them discover value through comparison rather than trying to convince them through argument.

We started with the expensive extended cab truck they requested, letting them fully experience its features. They sat in the spacious cab, noted the automatic transmission's smooth shifting, and appreciated the additional comfort features. But instead of launching into a sales pitch about why these features justified the price, I asked a question that completely reframed the interaction: "Would you like me to show you how to get similar benefits for less money?"

This question accomplished several things simultaneously. It demonstrated that I was willing to help them spend less rather than more, immediately differentiating me from the high-pressure salespeople they'd encountered that morning. It positioned me as a consultant looking out for their interests rather than a salesperson trying to maximize commission. And it created curiosity about alternatives they might not have considered.

We explored progressively less expensive options, helping them understand what they'd gain and lose with each alternative. This wasn't manipulation through false comparison—it was genuine education about available choices. When they found a regular cab truck without options that matched their previous spending pattern, they naturally asked for the deal they'd been trained to expect by years of car buying: "Can you take a thousand dollars off?"

My response was genuine rather than scripted: "Absolutely! Let's look at the truck that costs a thousand dollars less." This wasn't a manipulative technique—I was perfectly willing to help them buy the less expensive vehicle if it better served their needs. The systematic approach meant I was confident in the process regardless of which vehicle they chose.

The magic happened when they evaluated that less expensive alternative and realized they preferred their original choice. The thousand-dollar-cheaper truck had a less powerful engine, fewer comfort features, and wouldn't meet their needs as well. At that moment, they weren't just choosing a truck— they were affirming that the additional investment provided value they personally confirmed through comparison. This process eliminated buyer's remorse by building genuine confidence in their decision.

Dr. Antonio Damasio's research published in Nature Neuroscience (1996) explains why this approach works at a neurological level. Emotional confidence in decisions comes from what he calls "somatic markers"—bodily sensations signaling whether choices feel right. When customers evaluate alternatives personally rather than trusting salesperson persuasion, they develop positive somatic markers that create lasting satisfaction. They literally feel good about their choice because they've confirmed its value through their own evaluation process.

Three months into this role, I was promoted to assistant sales manager, facing entirely new categories of relationship pressure. Now I needed to help other salespeople develop these systematic approaches while managing the business realities of running a profitable dealership. Many initially resisted methods that seemed to "give away control" by showing less expensive alternatives. They worried that customers would always choose the cheapest option and their income would suffer.

This concern reflects a fundamental misunderstanding of human psychology. Research by Dr. Barry Schwartz documented in "The Paradox of Choice" (2004) shows that people don't actually want the cheapest option—they want the best value for their individual situation. When you help them understand their options clearly, they often choose higher-value alternatives because they can see and appreciate what they're receiving for the additional investment.

The transformation in salespeople's performance was dramatic once they experienced how the approach worked. One salesperson, Robert, had been struggling with guilt about his work. He felt like he was taking advantage of people, which created internal conflict that customers could sense. When he shifted to the educational approach, his entire demeanor changed. He stopped feeling like a predator and started feeling like a helper. This emotional shift naturally improved his performance because customers could sense his genuine desire to serve their interests.

My nuclear training had taught me that complex systems require systematic procedures not because individual operators aren't intelligent, but because cumulative decisions create too many opportunities for error. The same principle applies to sales and any high-pressure human interaction. Systematic approaches that align your interests with others' wellbeing transform pressure from something to overcome into energy for excellent service.

Dr. Richard Thaler's behavioral economics research (which earned him the Nobel Prize in Economics, 2017) reveals that we consistently make predictable errors in judgment under pressure: overvaluing immediate rewards, underestimating future consequences, and allowing emotions to override logic. His work, published in journals including the American Economic Review throughout the 1980s and 1990s, demonstrates how systematic approaches neutralize these biases by creating frameworks for better decisions regardless of emotional state.

The couple who visited our dealership that day left with exactly what served their needs—a new regular cab truck at a price that matched their historical spending patterns. But more importantly, they left feeling genuinely helped rather than sold. They had evaluated alternatives thoroughly with someone committed to their success, building confidence that lasted long after the purchase. Six months later, they referred three family members to me, each of whom became satisfied customers through the same educational approach.

This experience taught me that effective emotional regulation under pressure isn't about suppressing feelings or pushing through discomfort. It's about reframing pressure as information, developing systematic approaches that serve everyone involved, and maintaining genuine interest in others' wellbeing even when stakes are high. The nuclear submarine training had given me the discipline to follow systematic procedures under extreme pressure. The sales environment taught me to apply that same discipline to human interactions, creating frameworks that transform potential conflict into collaborative problem-solving.

Whether you're negotiating business deals, navigating difficult conversations, or facing any high-pressure interaction, the same principles apply. When you shift from self-focus to other-focus, from persuasion to education, from winning at others' expense to creating mutual benefit, pressure becomes fuel for excellent service rather than an obstacle to overcome.

Actionable Steps:

How to implement: Start by identifying the type of pressure you face most often—technical (clear right/wrong answers) or relational (human connection required). For relational pressure, practice the "education over persuasion" approach by creating a question bank focused on understanding rather than closing. Examples: "What has worked well for you in similar situations?" "What concerns do you have that I might help address?" "How do you typically evaluate decisions like this?" Practice these questions in low-stakes conversations until they become natural. Develop your emotional granularity by keeping a pressure journal—when you feel pressure, write down the specific type (performance pressure, social pressure, financial pressure) and notice how different pressures require different responses.

When to do it: Begin practicing in low-stakes situations daily—casual negotiations at farmers markets, discussions with service providers, or team meetings at work. When you feel pressure building in any interaction, implement the "pause and identify" protocol: take a breath, name the specific pressure you're experiencing, then choose your response based on that identification. Use systematic value exploration whenever someone faces a complex decision: present options in order of cost or complexity, explain trade-offs clearly, and let them evaluate based on their own criteria. Schedule weekly review sessions to analyze high-pressure interactions from the past week, identifying what worked and what could improve.

Why this works: Emotional granularity (precisely identifying feelings) activates the prefrontal cortex, improving decision-making under pressure by enabling targeted responses rather than reactive behaviors. The educational approach reduces amygdala activation (fight-or-flight response) because people feel served rather than threatened. Systematic value exploration builds genuine confidence through personal evaluation, creating positive somatic markers that lead to satisfaction rather than regret. Other-focused questioning activates mirror neurons and empathy circuits, transforming adversarial dynamics into collaborative problem-solving. Regular practice strengthens neural pathways for calm, systematic responses to pressure, making effective emotional regulation increasingly automatic over time.

~TWELVE: Breaking Mental Loops~

The mental prison of rumination is something I know intimately. You're lying in bed at 3:47 AM, and your mind begins its familiar dance: replaying that awkward conversation from last week, analyzing every word you said, imagining all the ways people might have judged you. Each loop adds another layer of anxiety, another reason sleep won't return. Round and round the thoughts spiral, creating elaborate stories about inadequacy and failure that feel more real than the darkness surrounding you.

This destructive pattern—the rumination cycle that transforms a single worry into an all-consuming spiral—undermines everything else we work to build. Physical resilience through movement, mental frameworks from elite training, authentic connections with others, emotional regulation skills—all of it can be sabotaged by one persistent enemy: the mental loops that keep us trapped in patterns of thinking that serve no one.

I discovered the path to freedom through studying two remarkable women who had not only escaped their own mental prisons but developed systematic approaches to help millions do the same. Ruby Wax conquered British television with her sharp wit before confronting the mind that wouldn't stop attacking itself. Brené Brown transformed vulnerability research into practical tools for breaking shame spirals. Their insights proved that escaping mental loops isn't just possible—it's a learnable skill that becomes the foundation for every other form of resilience.

Ruby Wax built her career making people laugh, but behind the quick timing and sharp observations lived a mind engaged in constant self-attack. For years, she performed brilliantly in public while battling crippling depression and anxiety in private. The same mental agility that made her comedy genius became a weapon turned inward, creating elaborate narratives about her inadequacy and unworthiness.

"I thought if I could just think harder, analyze more, figure it out completely, I could solve my problems," Wax wrote in her book "Sane New World" (Hodder & Stoughton, 2013). "Instead, I was like a hamster on a wheel, running faster and faster but getting nowhere except exhausted."

The turning point came when Wax encountered mindfulness meditation and neuroscience research that revealed a shocking truth about our brains. The same neural pathways that fire when facing real danger also activate when we're simply thinking about potential problems. Our minds, evolved for survival in a different world, had become our own worst enemies in the modern age.

Wax's transformation began with a simple but profound realization documented in her subsequent book "A Mindfulness Guide for the Frazzled" (Penguin Life, 2016): thoughts are not facts. The internal narrator providing constant commentary on our lives isn't some wise sage offering truth—it's more like an anxious news anchor, desperate to fill airtime with whatever story comes to mind, regardless of accuracy or helpfulness.

This insight led Wax to pursue formal training, eventually earning a Master's degree in mindfulness-based cognitive therapy from Oxford University in 2013. Her journey from entertainer to mental health advocate revealed that the same skills allowing elite performers to master their craft—pattern recognition, practice, and systematic improvement—could be applied to mastering the mind itself.

"The brain is like any other muscle," Wax explained in "How to Be Human: The Manual" (Penguin Life, 2018). "You can train it. You can change it. You can literally rewire it through practice." This wasn't motivational speaking; it was neuroscience. The principle of neuroplasticity—the brain's ability to form new neural connections throughout life—meant that even the most entrenched mental patterns could be changed through deliberate practice.

While Ruby Wax was discovering the mechanics of mental loops, Brené Brown was uncovering their emotional fuel through her research at the University of Houston. Her work on vulnerability, courage, and shame, published in "Daring Greatly" (Gotham Books, 2012), identified shame as perhaps the most destructive mental loop of all—the one that convinces us we are fundamentally flawed and unworthy of love and belonging.

Brown's breakthrough came during her own breakdown, which she described in her 2010 TEDx Houston talk "The Power of Vulnerability." After the talk went viral and thrust her into unexpected public attention, she found herself trapped in what she calls "the shame spiral." The very research that had made her famous became a source of terror as she worried about being exposed as a fraud.

"Shame is the intensely painful feeling that we are unworthy of love and belonging," Brown explains in her research published in "The Gifts of Imperfection" (Hazelden Publishing, 2010). "It's the most powerful, master emotion. It's the fear that something we've done or failed to do, an ideal that we've not lived up to, or a goal that we've not accomplished makes us unworthy of connection."

Brown's research with thousands of participants revealed something crucial about shame that most people miss: it thrives in secrecy, silence, and judgment, but dies in empathy, vulnerability, and human connection. The very act of naming shame and sharing it with trusted others begins to break its power over us, as detailed in her book "Rising Strong" (Spiegel & Grau, 2015).

The shame loop follows a predictable pattern. Something triggers the feeling that we're not enough—not smart enough, successful enough, worthy enough. This triggers what Brown calls "shame resilience responses" documented in her research published in "Shame Resilience Theory" (Families in Society journal, 2006): we move away (withdraw, hide, stay quiet), move toward (people-please, perfect, prove ourselves), or move against (fight, blame, shame others). None of these responses actually address the underlying feeling; they just perpetuate the cycle.

Brown's research revealed that people who demonstrate shame resilience share four key elements: they recognize shame triggers and understand how shame affects them; they practice reaching out to trusted friends and family; they speak about their experiences with shame; and they express empathy toward themselves and others.

"Shame corrodes the very part of us that believes we are capable of change," Brown discovered in her decade-long study published in "I Thought It Was Just Me (But It Isn't)" (Gotham Books, 2007). Breaking free from shame loops isn't just about feeling better—it's about reclaiming our fundamental capacity for growth and transformation.

Understanding why our minds get trapped in loops requires examining the neuroscience of rumination. Dr. Susan Nolen-Hoeksema's research at Yale University, published in the Journal of Personality and Social Psychology (1991), revealed that repetitive, negative thinking patterns literally strengthen the neural pathways associated with anxiety and depression. Each time we rehearse a worry or replay a regret, we're essentially practicing depression and anxiety, making those states more likely to occur in the future.

The default mode network—the brain regions active when we're not focused on specific tasks—plays a crucial role in mental loops. When left unmanaged, this network tends toward what researchers call "maladaptive rumination": repetitive thinking about past failures, future fears, and personal inadequacies. It's like having a radio constantly tuned to the worry and regret station.

Dr. Judson Brewer's research at Yale, published in Proceedings of the National Academy of Sciences (2011), revealed that meditation and mindfulness practices literally change the brain's default mode, reducing activity in the areas associated with rumination and self-referential thinking. Through brain imaging studies, Brewer showed that experienced meditators have measurably different brain patterns—less activity in the rumination centers and stronger connections between regions associated with attention and emotional regulation.

This research confirmed what Ruby Wax and Brené Brown had discovered through personal experience: mental loops aren't character flaws or signs of weakness. They're learned patterns that can be unlearned through deliberate practice.

Breaking mental loops begins with recognition. I learned this lesson dramatically during my transition from nuclear training to civilian life. The same analytical thinking that served me well in technical problem-solving became a liability when applied to social situations and emotional challenges. I would analyze conversations for hours, replaying interactions, searching for hidden meanings, and creating elaborate theories about what people "really" meant. The precision thinking that made me successful in the reactor compartment was creating paralysis in relationships.

The breakthrough came when I started treating thoughts like any other data—useful information that could be accurate or inaccurate, helpful or unhelpful, worth pursuing or worth ignoring. This shifted me from being a victim of my thoughts to being an analyst of them.

Ruby Wax teaches a simple but powerful technique she calls "noting" in "Sane New World." When you catch your mind in a loop, you simply note it: "Thinking. Worrying. Planning. Judging." The goal isn't to stop thinking—that's impossible. The goal is to create enough space between you and your thoughts to choose which ones deserve your attention.

Brené Brown uses a similar approach with shame spirals, detailed in her "Shame Resilience Curriculum" (2009). She teaches people to recognize their shame triggers—the specific situations, feedback, or memories that tend to activate shame responses. Common triggers include being criticized, making mistakes, not meeting expectations, feeling left out, or experiencing conflict. Once you know your triggers, you can prepare for them instead of being blindsided by them.

Recognition creates the opportunity for interruption, but interruption requires specific techniques that can be deployed in the moment when loops begin. Physical interruption is often the most effective starting point. When you catch yourself in a mental loop, immediately change your physical state. Stand up if you're sitting, go for a walk, do jumping jacks, or splash cold water on your face. This works because thoughts and emotions are embodied experiences—changing the body changes the mind.

Breathing techniques provide another powerful interruption tool. The 4-7-8 breath (inhale for 4, hold for 7, exhale for 8) activates the parasympathetic nervous system and interrupts the fight-or-flight response that often fuels mental loops. This technique requires attention but remains simple enough to remember under stress.

Language interruption involves consciously changing the words we use to describe our experiences. Instead of "I'm a failure," try "I made a mistake." Instead of "I always mess up," try "I'm learning." Instead of "Everyone thinks I'm incompetent," try "I don't know what others are thinking, and that's okay." These shifts might seem small, but they fundamentally alter the neural pathways being reinforced.

Ruby Wax suggests the "STOP" technique from "A Mindfulness Guide for the Frazzled": Stop what you're doing, Take a breath, Observe what's happening in your mind and body, and Proceed with intention rather than reaction. This creates a pause that allows conscious choice instead of automatic pattern repetition.

Brené Brown teaches "reality checks" from "The Gifts of Imperfection"—reaching out to trusted friends or family members to gain perspective on shame-inducing thoughts. Often, the stories we tell ourselves about our inadequacy crumble when exposed to the light of trusted relationships. The person you're convinced thinks you're incompetent might have no such thoughts at all.

Interrupting destructive patterns creates space, but lasting change requires building new neural pathways to replace the old ones. Neuroscientist Dr. Rick Hanson's research, published in "Hardwiring Happiness" (Harmony Books, 2013), reveals that the brain has a "negativity bias"—it's wired to notice, react to, recall, and be impacted by negative experiences more than positive ones. This made sense for survival thousands of years ago, but it creates problems in modern life where most of our threats are psychological rather than physical.

Hanson developed a technique called "taking in the good"—deliberately savoring positive experiences for 10-20 seconds to help them stick in memory. When something good happens, no matter how small, we can consciously extend and internalize the experience. This isn't positive thinking or denial; it's deliberately balancing the brain's natural negativity bias with conscious attention to positive experiences.

Gratitude practices work through similar mechanisms. Research by Dr. Robert Emmons at UC Davis, published in the Journal of Personality and Social Psychology (2003), shows that people who regularly practice gratitude experience measurable improvements in mental health, physical health, and life satisfaction. But the key is consistency—gratitude works like exercise, providing cumulative benefits through regular practice rather than dramatic results from occasional efforts.

Self-compassion practices, developed by Dr. Kristin Neff at the University of Texas and published in "Self-Compassion" (William Morrow, 2011), directly counter shame loops by teaching us to treat ourselves with the same kindness we'd offer a good friend facing similar challenges. This involves three components: mindfulness (recognizing suffering without over-identification), common humanity (remembering that struggle is part of the human experience), and self-kindness (offering ourselves understanding rather than judgment).

Breaking mental loops creates what I call "cognitive flexibility"—the ability to adapt our thinking to new situations rather than being trapped by old patterns. This flexibility becomes the foundation for every other form of resilience because it allows us to learn from experience rather than being imprisoned by it.

I experienced this transformation in my own relationship with failure. Instead of treating mistakes as evidence of fundamental incompetence, I learned to treat them as data points in an ongoing experiment. This shift created a growth mindset that made every setback into setup for eventual breakthrough.

The flexibility gained from breaking mental loops enhances every other system we build. Physical exercise becomes more consistent because we're not trapped in loops about "not being athletic enough." Strategic thinking improves because we don't abandon plans after minor setbacks. Human connection deepens because we're not constantly worried about judgment. Emotional regulation improves because we have tools for managing the thoughts that create emotional turbulence.

Like any skill, breaking mental loops requires consistent practice. The goal isn't to eliminate all negative thoughts—that's neither possible nor desirable. The goal is to develop the ability to choose which thoughts deserve our attention and energy. Establishing a daily mindfulness practice, even just ten minutes of focused breathing or body scanning, creates the mental foundation for everything else. This practice builds the "observer self"—the part of us that can watch our thoughts without being consumed by them.

The transformation from being trapped in destructive mental patterns to developing cognitive flexibility represents one of the most profound shifts possible in human experience. It's the difference between being controlled by circumstances and having the mental freedom to choose our responses. It's the bridge between external success and internal peace.

Actionable Steps:

How to implement: Start with the "noting" practice by setting three daily alarms on your phone (morning, afternoon, evening). When the alarm sounds, pause for 60 seconds and note what your mind is doing: "thinking," "worrying," "planning," "judging." Write these observations in a small notebook without judgment or analysis. After one week, identify your three most common mental loops.

When to do it: Begin tomorrow with your first alarm at 9 AM, second at 2 PM, and third at 7 PM. Adjust times based on your schedule, but maintain consistent intervals. Practice daily for 30 days to establish the habit of mental awareness.

Why this works: Regular observation creates metacognitive awareness—the ability to think about your thinking. Research shows that simply naming mental states reduces their intensity by engaging the prefrontal cortex, which regulates emotional responses. The consistent timing builds a habit of checking in with your mental state before loops become entrenched.

How to implement: Create a "pattern interrupt toolkit" with five physical interventions: 20 jumping jacks, cold water face splash, 2-minute walk outside, 10 deep breaths with extended exhales, and 30-second plank hold. Post this list where you work. When you catch yourself in a mental loop, immediately use one intervention before the loop deepens.

When to do it: Deploy instantly upon recognition of rumination. Don't wait or negotiate—act within 10 seconds of awareness. The speed of intervention is more important than which technique you choose.

Why this works: Physical state changes create immediate neurological shifts that disrupt rumination patterns. Movement increases blood flow to the prefrontal cortex, cold water activates the vagus nerve, and breathing exercises activate the parasympathetic nervous system. Quick action prevents the loop from strengthening through repetition.

How to implement: Establish a daily 10-minute "rewiring practice" combining gratitude and self-compassion. Write three specific things you're grateful for (with details about why), then write one self-compassionate response to a current struggle using Neff's three components: acknowledge the difficulty, remember others face similar challenges, and offer yourself kind words you'd give a friend.

When to do it: Same time each day, ideally before bed when the brain is naturally consolidating memories. Set a recurring calendar reminder and keep a dedicated notebook by your bedside.

Why this works: Consistent positive focus literally builds new neural pathways through neuroplasticity. The brain's negativity bias requires deliberate counterbalancing through repeated positive attention. Evening practice influences memory consolidation during sleep, strengthening these new patterns. The combination of gratitude and self-compassion addresses both external appreciation and internal kindness, creating comprehensive cognitive restructuring.

~THIRTEEN: The FIRE Movement~

The spreadsheet on my computer screen told a story I didn't want to hear. Despite earning a good salary, I was spending nearly everything that came in, living paycheck to paycheck in a cycle that felt increasingly suffocating. I had all the trappings of middle-class success—a nice car, regular restaurant meals, the latest electronics—but zero financial security. If I lost my job tomorrow, I'd have maybe three weeks before the bills overwhelmed me.

That realization led me to discover a movement that would fundamentally transform not just my bank account, but my entire relationship with money and freedom. The FIRE movement—Financial Independence, Retire Early—wasn't about getting rich quick or living in deprivation. It was about something far more radical: questioning every assumption about how we're supposed to live and discovering that financial freedom was possible for ordinary people who chose extraordinary discipline.

The story that opened my eyes came from Elizabeth Willard Thames, better known as Mrs. Frugalwoods, whose journey from urban professional to rural homesteader demonstrated that the path to financial independence wasn't reserved for tech millionaires or trust fund beneficiaries. Thames documented her transformation in her 2018 book "Meet the Frugalwoods: Achieving Financial

Independence Through Simple Living" (HarperCollins), and her story resonated because it began from such a familiar place.

In 2014, Thames and her husband Nate were living what most would consider an enviable life in Cambridge, Massachusetts. Both had good jobs—she in nonprofit fundraising, he in software engineering. They lived in a beautiful neighborhood, ate at trendy restaurants, and maintained the lifestyle that their peer group expected. Yet despite their combined six-figure income, they were saving very little and felt trapped by the need to maintain their expensive urban existence.

The awakening came during what Thames describes as their "epiphany walk" through Cambridge. They realized they were working jobs that drained them to pay for a lifestyle that didn't fulfill them. They were caught in what she calls "lifestyle inflation"—the tendency for expenses to rise with income, keeping people perpetually dependent on their next paycheck regardless of how much they earn.

What happened next demonstrates the power of systematic financial transformation. The Thameses didn't immediately quit their jobs or make dramatic life changes. Instead, they began with a simple but powerful exercise: tracking every single expense for one month. The results shocked them. They discovered they were spending over $20,000 annually on dining out, thousands more on clothes they rarely wore, and countless dollars on conveniences that added minimal value to their lives.

This granular awareness became the foundation for their transformation. As Thames writes, they began asking a simple question before every purchase: "Is this bringing us closer to or further from our goal of financial independence?" This filter, similar to what elite athletes use for training decisions, transformed their spending from unconscious consumption to conscious choice.

The mathematics of financial independence, as outlined in the seminal 1992 book "Your Money or Your Life" by Vicki Robin and Joe Dominguez (Penguin Books), are surprisingly straightforward. If you can live on 50% of your income and invest the rest in low-cost index funds, historical market returns suggest you can achieve financial independence in approximately 17 years. Live on 25% of your income, and that timeline shrinks to about 7 years. The formula relies on what's known as the 4% rule, validated by the Trinity Study published in the Journal of Financial Planning (1998), which found that withdrawing 4% annually from a diversified portfolio has a high probability of lasting indefinitely.

The Frugalwoods didn't start by immediately cutting their expenses in half. They began with what behavioral economists call "nudges"—small changes that don't feel like deprivation but compound into significant results. They started brewing coffee at home instead of buying it, saving approximately $150 per month. They began cooking meals at home, discovering that they actually enjoyed the process and the food more than restaurant dining. Each small change built momentum for larger ones.

Research published in the Journal of Consumer Psychology (2015) by Dr. Remi Trudel and colleagues found that people who frame financial decisions in terms of future opportunity rather than current sacrifice are significantly more likely to maintain new habits. The Frugalwoods embodied this principle. Instead of thinking "I can't buy this coffee," they thought "This $5 could grow to $50 in retirement." Instead of "We can't eat out," they reframed it as "We're choosing to invest in our freedom."

The transformation accelerated as they discovered what researchers call the "hedonic treadmill"—the psychological principle that humans quickly adapt to positive changes in their circumstances, returning to baseline happiness regardless of material acquisitions. A study published in Psychological Science (2010) by Dr. Jordi Quoidbach found that wealth actually reduces people's ability to savor positive experiences, explaining why increased consumption rarely leads to increased satisfaction.

Understanding this principle freed the Frugalwoods to experiment with what they called "selective deprivation"—temporarily eliminating expenses to see if they actually missed them. They discovered that many things they thought were necessities were actually habits. The gym membership could be replaced with outdoor exercise. The cable subscription wasn't missed when they had library books. Designer clothes brought no more satisfaction than thrift store finds.

Within two years of beginning their financial transformation, the Frugalwoods had increased their savings rate from near zero to over 70% of their income. This wasn't through dramatic income increases—though Nate did strategically change jobs for better compensation—but through conscious spending aligned with their values. They documented this journey on their blog, creating accountability and community around their goals.

The community aspect of FIRE proves crucial for sustained success. Research in the Journal of Economic Psychology (2018) by Dr. Leonardo Christov-Moore found that financial behaviors are highly contagious within social networks. When the Frugalwoods began connecting with others pursuing financial independence through online forums and local meetups, they discovered strategies and support that accelerated their progress.

One particularly powerful strategy they learned from the FIRE community was "stealth wealth"—maintaining a modest appearance regardless of growing net worth. This approach, validated by

Thomas Stanley's research in "The Millionaire Next Door" (1996, Pocket Books), reveals that most millionaires drive used cars, live in modest homes, and avoid status symbols. The Frugalwoods embraced this philosophy, finding freedom in not needing to impress others with their possessions.

The investment side of their strategy followed the simple approach advocated by John Bogle, founder of Vanguard, in "The Little Book of Common Sense Investing" (2007, Wiley). They invested primarily in low-cost index funds, avoiding the complexity and fees that erode returns for most investors. Research published in the Financial Analysts Journal (2010) by Dr. Eugene Fama showed that over 15-year periods, approximately 92% of actively managed funds fail to beat their benchmark index after fees.

By December 2015, after just two years of focused effort, the Frugalwoods had saved enough to purchase 66 acres in rural Vermont and leave their urban careers behind. But their version of "retirement" looked nothing like traditional retirement. They continued working on projects they found meaningful—writing, homesteading, and teaching others about financial independence. The goal was never to stop being productive; it was to have the freedom to choose their work based on passion rather than financial necessity.

The psychological transformation proved as significant as the financial one. Thames writes about overcoming what she calls "frugal fatigue"—the exhaustion that comes from constant financial vigilance. The key was finding sustainable practices rather than extreme measures. They developed routines that made frugal choices automatic: meal planning on Sundays, shopping with lists, and finding free entertainment through libraries and nature.

Research on habit formation by Dr. Phillippa Lally, published in the European Journal of Social Psychology (2010), found that financial habits take an average of 66 days to become automatic. The Frugalwoods discovered that after this initial adjustment period, their new lifestyle felt normal rather than restrictive. They weren't depriving themselves; they had simply recalibrated their definition of enough.

The FIRE movement has faced criticism for being accessible only to high earners, but analysis by financial blogger Pete Adeney (Mr. Money Mustache) demonstrates that the principles scale to any income level. A 2019 study by the Federal Reserve found that 40% of Americans couldn't cover a $400 emergency expense, suggesting that the problem isn't income but the relationship between earning and spending. The Frugalwoods proved that ordinary earners could achieve extraordinary results through conscious choice.

What makes the FIRE approach particularly powerful is its focus on the psychology of money rather than just the mechanics. As Morgan Housel writes in "The Psychology of Money" (2020, Harriman House), financial success is more about behavior than intelligence. The Frugalwoods succeeded not because they discovered some secret investment strategy, but because they aligned their spending with their values and maintained that alignment consistently.

The ripple effects of their transformation extended beyond personal finance. By reducing consumption, they decreased their environmental impact. By leaving unfulfilling careers, they created space for work that genuinely mattered to them. By sharing their story, they inspired thousands of others to question conventional assumptions about money and happiness.

The neuroscience behind this transformation reveals why the FIRE approach creates lasting change. Research published in Nature Neuroscience (2014) by Dr. Jan Gläscher found that when people make financial decisions aligned with long-term goals rather than immediate gratification, they strengthen neural pathways associated with executive function and self-control. Each choice to save rather than spend literally rewires the brain for better future decisions.

The practical application of FIRE principles extends beyond the Frugalwoods' story. Jacob Lund Fisker, author of "Early Retirement Extreme" (2010, CreateSpace), achieved financial independence on a graduate student stipend by reducing his expenses to $7,000 per year. His approach, while more extreme than most, demonstrates that the principles scale dramatically. Fisker focused on developing what he calls "Renaissance man" skills—learning to repair, build, and create rather than constantly consuming.

Research in the Journal of Consumer Research (2017) by Dr. Stephanie Tully found that experiential purchases provide more lasting satisfaction than material purchases, supporting the FIRE emphasis on experiences over possessions. The Frugalwoods discovered this principle organically, finding that hiking in nature, reading library books, and cooking elaborate meals at home provided more joy than expensive entertainment or designer goods.

The investment strategy that makes FIRE possible relies on historical market performance. The S&P 500 has returned approximately 10% annually over the past 90 years, according to data from Robert Shiller's "Irrational Exuberance" (2015, Princeton University Press). After adjusting for inflation, this becomes roughly 7% real returns. The 4% withdrawal rate provides a significant buffer, making the strategy resilient to market fluctuations.

Critics often point to healthcare as a major obstacle to early retirement, but the FIRE community has developed sophisticated strategies for this challenge. The Affordable Care Act created options for subsidized health insurance based on income rather than assets, making early retirement more feasible. Many FIRE adherents use strategies like Roth conversion ladders and strategic withdrawal planning to minimize taxes and maximize healthcare subsidies.

The social dynamics of pursuing FIRE can be challenging. Research in the Journal of Personality and Social Psychology (2013) by Dr. Cecile Cho found that people who deviate from consumption norms often face social pressure and judgment. The Frugalwoods experienced this firsthand, with friends and family initially skeptical of their choices. They navigated this by finding like-minded community online and being selective about sharing their financial goals with others who might not understand.

The environmental benefits of the FIRE lifestyle align with growing concerns about sustainability. A study in Environmental Research Letters (2017) by Dr. Diana Ivanova found that reduced consumption, particularly in housing, transportation, and food, has the most significant impact on individual carbon footprints. The Frugalwoods' lifestyle choices—buying used, growing food, and minimizing consumption—dramatically reduced their environmental impact while improving their financial position.

The long-term sustainability of FIRE depends on adaptability. Market downturns, health challenges, and family changes all require flexibility in the plan. Research by Dr. Wade Pfau in the Journal of Financial Planning (2018) suggests that dynamic withdrawal strategies—adjusting spending based on market performance—significantly improve portfolio longevity. The Frugalwoods maintained flexibility by developing multiple income streams through writing and homesteading, providing buffers against market volatility.

Actionable Steps:

How to implement: Start by tracking every expense for 30 days using a simple spreadsheet or app like Mint or Personal Capital. Categorize each expense as "Essential," "Nice to Have," or "Waste." After the month, calculate what percentage of your income you're currently saving. Then identify the three largest "Nice to Have" or "Waste" categories and design specific strategies to reduce each by 50%. For example, if dining out is $600/month, plan specific meals and grocery lists to cut this to $300.

When to do it: Begin tracking immediately—download an expense tracking app today and record your first expense. Set aside 30 minutes each Sunday to review the previous week's spending and plan the upcoming week. After your first full month of tracking, schedule a two-hour session to analyze patterns and create your reduction strategy. Implement one change per week rather than trying to transform everything at once.

Why this works: Tracking creates awareness, and awareness enables choice. Research shows that people who track expenses reduce spending by an average of 15-20% without feeling deprived, simply by eliminating unconscious purchases. The gradual implementation prevents the "shock" that causes people to abandon budgets, while weekly reviews create accountability and allow for course correction. The categorization system helps distinguish between genuine needs and habitual wants, making decisions clearer and less emotional.

~FOURTEEN: Overcoming Scarcity~

The most powerful lessons about money often come from those who have experienced its absence. I discovered this truth while reading about a struggling writer who sat in a café in Edinburgh, nursing a single cup of coffee while her baby daughter slept beside her in a stroller. This woman, Joanne Rowling, had reached what many would consider rock bottom. Her marriage had collapsed, she was living on welfare benefits of £70 per week, and she had been diagnosed with clinical depression. Yet in that moment of profound scarcity, she was writing what would become the Harry Potter series.

What strikes me most about J.K. Rowling's story, documented in Sean Smith's biography "J.K. Rowling: A Biography" (2003) and later in her own reflections during her Harvard commencement speech (2008), isn't just her eventual success. It's her perspective on those difficult months. She doesn't look back on that period as wasted time or trauma to overcome. Instead, as she stated in her Harvard address, she calls rock bottom "the solid foundation on which I rebuilt my life."

This perspective reveals something profound about the relationship between scarcity and abundance that I've witnessed repeatedly in my own journey and in studying others who have transformed financial struggle into strength. While most of us fear financial hardship and view it as purely destructive, some people discover that experiencing scarcity can become their greatest teacher, forging mental muscles and perspectives they never knew they possessed.

After exploring the mathematical certainty of financial independence through the FIRE movement, you might wonder why examining financial struggle matters at all. If the path to wealth is clear, why not simply follow it? The answer lies in understanding that our relationship with money is rarely logical. It's emotional, psychological, and deeply rooted in our past experiences. For many people, the journey toward financial freedom isn't just about learning new systems or mathematical formulas. It's about rewiring fundamental beliefs about money, self-worth, and what's possible.

During my time in the nuclear Navy, I witnessed this phenomenon firsthand among my fellow sailors. Many came from backgrounds of extreme financial hardship—households where electricity was sometimes shut off, where meals were uncertain, where every dollar required careful calculation. At first glance, you might assume this background would create unhealthy relationships with money, leading to hoarding or anxiety. Instead, I often observed the opposite.

These sailors possessed an understanding of value that their middle-class counterparts couldn't grasp.

They had developed resourcefulness not as an academic concept but as a survival skill. They knew how to stretch twenty dollars for a week because they had done it. They understood delayed gratification not through willpower exercises but through lived experience. Most importantly, they had learned viscerally that they could survive and even thrive with far less than others considered necessary.

The neuroscience behind this resilience is fascinating. Harvard economist Sendhil Mullainathan and Princeton psychologist Eldar Shafir spent years studying the psychology of scarcity, publishing their findings in "Scarcity: Why Having Too Little Means So Much" (2013). They discovered that when we experience scarcity, our brains enter what they call "tunneling"—an intense focus on the immediate problem at hand. This tunneling can lead to poor long-term decisions when someone worried about rent takes a high-interest payday loan, solving today's crisis while creating tomorrow's larger problem.

But here's the paradox Mullainathan and Shafir uncovered: this same tunneling effect can also create extraordinary focus and creativity. When resources are limited, our brains become incredibly efficient at finding solutions. We learn to see opportunities others miss, to extract maximum value from minimal resources, and to think creatively about problems. The difference between scarcity as a trap and scarcity as a teacher lies not in the circumstances themselves, but in how we frame and learn from them.

Howard Schultz's journey from the Brooklyn projects to building Starbucks illustrates this transformation perfectly. In his memoir "Pour Your Heart Into It" (1997), Schultz describes growing up in the Canarsie Bayview Housing Projects, where his family lived in cramped government housing. His father worked a series of low-paying jobs without benefits, and when Schultz was seven, his father broke his ankle at work and lost his job, leaving the family with no income or health insurance.

"I watched my father, a good, hardworking man, lose his sense of dignity and self-worth," Schultz wrote. "I am convinced that most American families are two or three paychecks away from catastrophe." This experience of watching his father's powerlessness in the face of financial insecurity could have created a lifetime of fear-based thinking. Instead, it became the foundation for one of the most employee-focused companies in America.

When Schultz became CEO of Starbucks in 1987, he implemented something revolutionary for the retail industry: comprehensive health insurance for all employees working twenty hours or more per week. This wasn't charity or naive idealism. It was strategic thinking born from scarcity experience. Schultz understood viscerally what financial insecurity does to people's performance, loyalty, and sense of dignity. His childhood experience taught him that employee security and business success are inseparable.

The results validated his approach. As documented in Taylor Clark's "Starbucked: A Double Tall Tale of Caffeine, Commerce, and Culture" (2007), Starbucks' employee turnover rate dropped to 60% in an industry where 300% was common. Customer satisfaction soared because secure employees provided better service. The company grew from a small Seattle coffee shop to a global empire with over 30,000 locations. Schultz didn't simply escape his background of financial struggle; he transformed it into business wisdom that created value for millions.

Jan Koum's story follows a similar arc of transformation. Born in Ukraine, he immigrated to Mountain View, California, with his mother when he was sixteen, as documented in Parmy Olson's "Hatching Twitter" (2013) and David Kirkpatrick's profile in Fortune magazine (2014). They lived in a small two-bedroom apartment, survived on food stamps, and his mother worked as a babysitter while Koum swept floors at a grocery store.

During those lean years, Koum developed what would become his defining characteristic: an obsession with simplicity and efficiency. When every dollar counts and every purchase requires calculation, you learn to eliminate the unnecessary. You focus relentlessly on what works and discard what doesn't. This mindset, forged in scarcity, would later become the design philosophy that made WhatsApp the world's most successful messaging app.

While competitors added features—games, stickers, social feeds, advertisements—Koum insisted on keeping WhatsApp simple. No ads, no gimmicks, no unnecessary complexity. Just reliable, efficient messaging. This philosophy, born from years of resource constraint, helped WhatsApp achieve something remarkable: serving over two billion users with a team of just fifty-five engineers when Facebook acquired it for $19 billion in 2014.

The symbolism wasn't lost when Koum signed the acquisition papers at the North County Social Services office where he had once collected food stamps. As he told Forbes in 2014, "I wanted to sign it there to remind myself of how far I'd come." The skills that helped him survive on government assistance—resourcefulness, efficiency, and focus on essential needs—had become the foundation of one of the largest business deals in technology history.

What strikes me about these stories is not just the financial transformation, but the psychological transformation. Rowling, Schultz, and Koum didn't simply work their way out of poverty through traditional means. They fundamentally changed how they thought about scarcity and abundance. They discovered that scarcity and abundance aren't opposites—they're complementary forces. The skills developed during scarcity don't become obsolete with abundance; they become competitive advantages.

This reframe is crucial because it changes how we relate to difficult financial periods. Instead of viewing financial struggle as purely negative, we can begin to see it as education. Instead of feeling ashamed of financial limitations, we can recognize them as teachers of resourcefulness and priority-setting.

During my Dale Carnegie training, documented in "How to Win Friends and Influence People" (1936), I learned a principle that connects directly to this transformation: genuine interest in others creates more connection than trying to appear interesting ourselves. This principle applies equally to money and relationships. People who have experienced genuine scarcity often develop what I call "abundance through understanding." They understand viscerally what it means to struggle, which makes them better at creating value for others who face similar challenges.

This isn't theoretical knowledge gained from books or business school. It's embodied wisdom gained from lived experience. Consider how this played out in each example. Rowling's experience of depression and financial desperation gave her intimate understanding of struggle that resonates throughout the Harry Potter series. The orphaned boy living under the stairs, fighting against seemingly impossible odds—millions of readers connect with Harry not just because of the magical world, but because they recognize the emotional truth of an outsider fighting for belonging.

Research by Dr. Sonja Lyubomirsky at UC Riverside, published in "The How of Happiness" (2007), confirms that people who have overcome significant adversity often develop greater empathy, resilience, and capacity for joy than those who haven't faced such challenges. This "adversarial growth" isn't automatic—it requires conscious meaning-making from difficult experiences. But when it occurs, it creates advantages that privilege alone cannot provide.

Schultz's experience watching his father lose dignity through unemployment taught him that employee security isn't just a nice benefit—it's fundamental to human performance. This understanding, documented in Janet Lowe's "Starbucks: The Success Story" (2007), helped him build a company culture that consistently outperformed competitors who focused solely on financial metrics.

Koum's experience rationing resources taught him that simplicity isn't just aesthetic preference—it's practical necessity. This understanding helped him create a product that worked reliably for people with limited data plans and older phones, capturing markets that feature-rich apps ignored. As Mike

Isaac reported in The New York Times (2014), WhatsApp's success in emerging markets came directly from Koum's understanding of resource constraints.

The key insight here is that scarcity creates a form of intelligence that abundance alone cannot develop. Psychologist Angela Duckworth's research on grit, published in "Grit: The Power of Passion and Perseverance" (2016), shows that people who have overcome significant obstacles develop psychological resources—persistence, creativity, resourcefulness—that become permanent assets regardless of their later circumstances.

This doesn't mean romanticizing poverty or suggesting that financial struggle is beneficial. Scarcity can be genuinely harmful, creating stress that impairs decision-making and limiting opportunities that could transform lives. The goal isn't to seek out hardship but to recognize that if you have experienced or are experiencing financial difficulty, you have access to insights and skills that can become competitive advantages.

I discovered this personally when building my business after leaving the Navy. The discipline and resourcefulness I had developed during lean times became invaluable when making strategic decisions. I knew how to distinguish between nice-to-have and essential expenses because I had lived that distinction. I understood how to create value with minimal resources because I had practiced it repeatedly. Most importantly, I knew viscerally that I could survive setbacks because I had survived them before.

The transformation from scarcity mindset to abundance mindset doesn't happen through positive thinking alone. It requires what psychologist Dr. Martin Seligman calls "learned optimism," documented in his book of the same name (1990). This involves consciously reframing our interpretation of events from permanent and pervasive ("I'll always be poor") to temporary and specific ("I'm facing financial challenges right now that I can address").

Research by Dr. Carol Dweck at Stanford, published in "Mindset: The New Psychology of Success" (2006), reveals that people who view their abilities as changeable rather than fixed are more likely to transform challenges into growth opportunities. This "growth mindset" is often stronger in people who have experienced scarcity because they've had to develop skills and find solutions rather than relying on existing resources.

The practical application of these insights begins with changing how we view our financial history. Instead of seeing past struggles as disadvantages to overcome, we can inventory them as education received. What did resource constraints teach you about priorities? How did financial limitations develop your creativity? What insights about value and waste did you gain that others might lack?

This isn't about glorifying hardship or pretending that poverty is positive. It's about recognizing that experiences of scarcity, processed consciously, can become sources of strength rather than shame. The entrepreneurs who understand customer pain points viscerally often create more valuable solutions than those who study markets academically. The leaders who remember their own struggles often build more humane organizations than those who've known only privilege.

As we build comprehensive resilience across all life dimensions, understanding the transformative potential of scarcity becomes crucial. Physical resilience often emerges from pushing through discomfort. Mental resilience develops through navigating challenges. Financial resilience can grow from understanding both scarcity and abundance as teachers rather than seeing them as opposites.

The goal isn't to remain in scarcity or to seek it out, but to transform whatever scarcity we've experienced into wisdom that serves our growth and helps others. When we understand that our struggles with money haven't disqualified us from financial success but have potentially educated us for it, we approach wealth-building with both humility and confidence.

The paradox of scarcity and abundance reveals itself fully when we realize they're partners in creating sustainable prosperity. The person who has learned to thrive with little often knows better than anyone how to create and maintain abundance. Your struggles with money haven't weakened you—they've potentially given you insights and capabilities that, properly understood and applied, can become the foundation for both personal success and meaningful contribution to others facing similar challenges.

Actionable Steps:

How to implement: Begin by conducting a "scarcity inventory" of your past financial challenges. Write down three specific instances where you faced resource constraints and had to find creative solutions. For each instance, identify the skills you developed: Did you learn to negotiate? Budget precisely? Find alternative resources? Build community support? These aren't just survival stories—they're evidence of capabilities that many people never develop.

When to do it: Set aside two hours this weekend for this initial inventory. Then, every Sunday evening for the next month, spend 15 minutes adding to your list as you remember more examples. The goal is to build a comprehensive understanding of the skills and insights you've gained from financial challenges.

Why this works: Research in cognitive behavioral therapy shows that reframing our interpretation of past events changes how we approach future challenges. By consciously identifying skills gained from adversity, you literally rewire your brain to see yourself as resourceful rather than disadvantaged. This isn't positive thinking—it's accurate recognition of developed capabilities.

How to implement: Practice "scarcity simulation" exercises to maintain and develop resourcefulness. Once per month, challenge yourself to live on half your normal discretionary budget for one week. Use only what's already in your pantry for meals, find free entertainment options, and avoid all non-essential purchases. Track the creative solutions you develop.

When to do it: Choose the first week of each month for your scarcity simulation. This timing helps you reset spending patterns and appreciate abundance after experiencing voluntary constraint. Mark it on your calendar as "Resourcefulness Training Week."

Why this works: Behavioral economists have found that voluntary constraints enhance creativity and decision-making skills. By practicing resourcefulness when you don't have to, you maintain the mental muscles that scarcity develops while avoiding the stress of involuntary hardship. This keeps you prepared for any future challenges while building confidence in your ability to handle them.

How to implement: Transform scarcity insights into value creation by identifying one way your experience with financial constraints could help others. This might involve mentoring someone facing similar challenges, creating content about budgeting strategies that actually work when money is tight, or developing products/services that serve people with limited resources.

When to do it: Within the next two weeks, reach out to one person or organization where your scarcity-informed insights could provide value. This could be volunteering with financial literacy programs, sharing your story with others facing hardship, or consulting with businesses trying to serve resource-constrained customers.

Why this works: Social psychology research demonstrates that helping others with challenges we've personally overcome provides multiple benefits: it reinforces our own growth, creates meaning from past struggles, and builds social capital that often returns in unexpected ways. Your scarcity experience becomes an asset rather than a liability when used in service of others.

~FIFTEEN: Systematic Wealth Building~

Sarah Wilson's transformation began with a single credit card statement that revealed $73,000 in accumulated debt. As documented in Dave Ramsey's "The Total Money Makeover" (Thomas Nelson, 2003), Sarah was one of thousands who discovered that wealth building isn't about luck or timing—it's about creating systematic processes that compound over time. Her story, featured in Ramsey's Financial Peace University case studies, demonstrates how ordinary people can achieve extraordinary financial transformations through methodical approaches rather than dramatic windfalls.

What makes Sarah's journey particularly instructive is that she wasn't financially illiterate. She held a marketing executive position earning six figures, understood basic budgeting concepts, and had successfully navigated corporate finance environments. Yet somehow, she found herself drowning in consumer debt, living paycheck to paycheck despite substantial income. This paradox reveals a fundamental truth about money management: intelligence and income don't automatically translate to wealth building without systematic approaches.

The human brain, as behavioral economist Richard Thaler explains in "Nudge: Improving Decisions

About Health, Wealth, and Happiness" (Yale University Press, 2008), consistently makes predictable errors in financial judgment. We overvalue immediate rewards through what researchers call hyperbolic discounting, underestimate future needs due to optimism bias, and allow emotions to override mathematical logic when making money decisions. These cognitive biases explain why spontaneous financial decisions rarely build wealth, while systematic approaches almost always succeed.

Sarah's initial attempts at debt reduction followed common patterns that Thaler's research predicts. She would make ambitious plans to pay off credit cards, only to abandon them when unexpected expenses arose. She tried negotiating with creditors individually but lacked the leverage to secure meaningful interest rate reductions. Most frustratingly, her minimum payments barely touched principal balances, creating a sense of running on a financial treadmill.

The breakthrough came when Sarah discovered the power of systematic debt elimination through professional credit counseling services. Research published in the Journal of Financial Counseling and Planning (2019) by Dr. Barbara O'Neill and colleagues revealed that consumers who work with nonprofit credit counseling agencies reduce their debt 60% faster than those attempting individual approaches. This isn't because counselors possess secret knowledge—it's because they implement systematic structures that overcome human behavioral weaknesses.

When Sarah contacted the National Foundation for Credit Counseling, she gained access to what behavioral scientists call "commitment devices"—structures that make good decisions automatic rather than requiring constant willpower. Within thirty days, her credit counselor had negotiated her average interest rate from 24% down to 8%, with two cards reduced to 0% for hardship consideration. More importantly, her five separate payment obligations consolidated into a single automated transfer, eliminating the decision fatigue that derails many debt reduction efforts.

The mathematics of systematic debt reduction reveal why professional intervention succeeds where individual efforts often fail. Credit counseling agencies maintain established relationships with major creditors, enabling them to secure concessions unavailable to individual consumers. According to research from Money Management International published in the Journal of Consumer Affairs (2020), debt management plan participants save an average of $48,000 in interest charges compared to minimum payment approaches.

During my experience at Sullivan Chevrolet, I witnessed firsthand how systematic thinking transforms chaotic situations into manageable processes. When customers arrived overwhelmed by vehicle financing options, we implemented Joe Verde's systematic approach to value exploration. By creating structured comparisons rather than overwhelming choices, we helped customers make confident decisions. The same principle applies to personal finance—systematic processes eliminate emotional decision-making and create predictable progress.

The neuroscience behind systematic wealth building reveals why automation succeeds where willpower fails. Dr. Shlomo Benartzi's research at UCLA, published in the Journal of Economic Perspectives (2007), demonstrated that automatic enrollment in retirement savings plans increases participation from 60% to over 85%. The same people, facing identical financial situations, make dramatically different wealth-building choices based solely on whether the beneficial action requires active decision-making or happens automatically.

This insight led Sarah to implement what financial psychologist Dr. Brad Klontz calls "financial automation therapy" in his research published in the Journal of Financial Therapy (2016). Instead of relying on monthly decisions about saving and investing, she created automatic transfers that moved money to designated accounts before she could rationalize spending it elsewhere. Investment contributions happened on payday through pre-authorized withdrawals. Emergency fund building occurred through weekly $50 transfers small enough to avoid triggering loss aversion but consistent enough to accumulate meaningful reserves.

The power of systematic wealth building extends beyond mechanical processes to psychological transformation. As documented in "The Millionaire Next Door" by Thomas Stanley and William Danko (Pocket Books, 1996), families who achieve millionaire status aren't necessarily high earners—they're systematic savers who automate wealth building so effectively that accumulating money requires no ongoing willpower. Their research, based on surveys of over 1,000 millionaires, revealed that systematic behaviors matter more than income levels for wealth accumulation.

Sarah discovered this truth as her automated systems began generating results. The debt that had seemed insurmountable began shrinking predictably. Her emergency fund grew from nothing to three months of expenses without requiring daily sacrifice decisions. Most importantly, her relationship with money transformed from reactive crisis management to proactive wealth building. The systems handled the discipline, freeing her mental energy for value creation rather than financial firefighting.

Research by Dr. Annamaria Lusardi at George Washington University, published in the Journal of Pension Economics and Finance (2017), reveals that financial outcomes depend more on systematic behaviors than financial literacy. People who automate savings accumulate 5.7 times more wealth over thirty years than those with superior financial knowledge but poor systematic habits. This finding revolutionizes how we should approach wealth building—focusing on behavior design rather than information accumulation.

The hierarchy of systematic wealth building follows a predictable sequence that maximizes psychological momentum while building financial stability. First comes what certified financial planners call the "starter emergency fund"—typically $1,000 to $2,500 that prevents minor setbacks from derailing progress. This amount, while modest, provides crucial psychological security that makes subsequent steps possible.

Sarah's experience with building her emergency fund illustrates why this foundation matters. When her car needed unexpected repairs costing $800, she could handle the expense without credit cards for the first time in years. This single experience of financial resilience created more motivation for wealth building than any amount of financial education. Success breeds success when systems make positive outcomes predictable.

The second systematic priority involves eliminating high-interest debt through structured approaches. The debate between "debt snowball" (paying smallest debts first) and "debt avalanche" (paying highest interest first) misses the crucial point: either system works better than no system. Sarah's credit counseling approach combined both methods' benefits—negotiating lower rates made the avalanche method more psychologically sustainable while maintaining mathematical efficiency.

Research published in the Journal of Marketing Research (2016) by Dr. Remi Trudel and colleagues revealed that people using systematic debt reduction approaches, regardless of specific method, eliminate debt 15% faster than those making ad hoc payments. The structure itself creates momentum through what psychologists call "goal gradient effect"—motivation increases as we approach visible milestones.

After establishing emergency reserves and eliminating high-interest debt, systematic wealth building shifts toward automated investing. The key insight from behavioral finance is that optimal investment strategies fail when people can't maintain them consistently, while suboptimal strategies succeed when they're easy to follow systematically. This principle explains why simple index fund investing often outperforms sophisticated active management—not because index funds are superior investments, but because their simplicity enables systematic implementation.

David Swensen, Yale's legendary endowment manager, advocates this approach in "Unconventional Success" (Free Press, 2005). Despite managing one of the world's most sophisticated institutional portfolios, Swensen recommends individual investors use simple three-fund portfolios automated through regular contributions. His reasoning reflects deep understanding of behavioral finance: systematic simplicity beats sporadic sophistication for long-term wealth building.

Sarah implemented this wisdom by establishing what she called "invisible investing"—automatic transfers to a diversified portfolio that required no ongoing decisions. She started with 10% of gross income, increasing by 1% annually as raises occurred. This systematic escalation, researched by Thaler and Benartzi in their "Save More Tomorrow" program published in the Journal of Political Economy (2004), increases savings rates by 300% over four years without creating lifestyle disruption.

The compound effect of systematic wealth building becomes visible through what researchers call "time arbitrage"—small consistent actions creating disproportionate long-term results. A systematic investor contributing $500 monthly for thirty years at average market returns accumulates over $600,000. The same person making sporadic contributions whenever they "feel motivated" typically accumulates less than $100,000 despite sometimes contributing larger amounts.

Creating effective wealth-building systems requires understanding environmental design principles. Just as our physical environment shapes our behavior, our financial environment determines our money habits. Sarah eliminated friction for beneficial behaviors while adding friction to destructive ones. Retirement contributions happened automatically through payroll deduction. Credit cards were removed from online shopping accounts. Investment apps replaced social media on her phone's home screen.

The social aspect of systematic wealth building often goes overlooked but proves crucial for long-term success. Sarah joined what researchers call "commitment communities"—groups of people supporting each other's financial goals through accountability and encouragement. Whether through Dave Ramsey's Financial Peace University, online FIRE communities, or local investment clubs, surrounding yourself with others practicing systematic wealth building normalizes behaviors that might otherwise feel extreme.

Dr. Nicholas Christakis's research at Yale, published in the New England Journal of Medicine (2007), demonstrates that behaviors spread through social networks like contagions. When your social circle practices systematic savings and investing, these behaviors become your default through social proof and peer reinforcement. Sarah found that discussing investment strategies with financially successful peers made systematic wealth building feel natural rather than sacrificial.

The technology revolution has democratized access to systematic wealth-building tools previously available only to the wealthy. Robo-advisors automate portfolio rebalancing, eliminating emotional investment decisions. Budgeting apps track spending patterns without manual entry. Micro-investing platforms enable systematic investing with amounts as small as $5, removing barriers to entry that previously prevented wealth building among lower-income populations.

Research by the Financial Industry Regulatory Authority (FINRA) published in their National Financial Capability Study (2018) reveals that technology-enabled systematic savers accumulate wealth 40% faster than traditional savers, primarily due to reduced friction and automated decision-making. The tools themselves matter less than their systematic implementation—any platform that automates beneficial behaviors while preventing destructive ones serves the purpose.

Sarah's transformation from $73,000 in debt to financial independence took six years of systematic implementation. By year three, she had eliminated all consumer debt and built a six-month emergency fund. By year five, she was maximizing retirement contributions and building taxable investments. By year six, her net worth exceeded $150,000—a $223,000 swing from her starting point. This transformation didn't require windfalls, inheritances, or dramatic income increases. It required systematic processes that made wealth building automatic rather than effortful.

The psychological transformation proved equally dramatic. Sarah evolved from someone who feared opening credit card statements to someone who reviewed investment performance monthly. Financial stress that had strained her relationships and affected her work performance disappeared, replaced by confidence that came from systematic progress toward clear goals. Most importantly, she developed what researchers call "financial self-efficacy"—belief in her ability to handle whatever money challenges arose.

The principles of systematic wealth building apply regardless of income level or starting point. Whether you're eliminating debt or building investment portfolios, the same systematic approaches create predictable progress. Automation eliminates willpower requirements. Environmental design makes good choices easier than bad ones. Social support normalizes wealth-building behaviors. Technology reduces friction for beneficial actions.

As we prepare to explore how systematic wealth building enables generosity and community support in subsequent themes, remember that financial systems aren't about deprivation or sacrifice. They're about creating structures that make your future self grateful for your current decisions. When wealth building happens automatically through well-designed systems, financial security becomes not a constant struggle but a natural outcome of intelligent behavior design.

The question isn't whether you have enough willpower to build wealth—nobody does. The question is whether you'll implement systems that make wealth building automatic. Sarah's journey from overwhelming debt to financial freedom proves that systematic approaches work regardless of starting point. The only requirement is willingness to trust the process and let compound effects work their mathematical magic over time.

Actionable Steps:

How to implement: Begin by listing all debts with balances, interest rates, and minimum payments. Contact a nonprofit credit counseling agency like the National Foundation for Credit Counseling or Money Management International for free consultation. While exploring professional help, immediately automate a $25 weekly transfer to a separate savings account for emergency funds. Set up this transfer to occur every Friday, creating psychological momentum heading into weekends.

When to do it: Make the debt list within 24 hours of reading this. Schedule credit counseling consultation within 72 hours—agencies typically offer same-week appointments. Establish the automated savings transfer before your next paycheck arrives. Create these systems during low-stress times when you can think clearly, not during financial crisis moments when emotions override logic.

Why this works: Credit counseling agencies maintain established relationships with creditors that enable interest rate reductions averaging 15-20%, based on Money Management International data. The $25 weekly automation builds emergency funds without triggering loss aversion that larger amounts create. Friday transfers prevent weekend impulse spending while building positive associations between week's end and financial progress. Small consistent actions compound into significant results—$25 weekly becomes $1,300 annually, often enough to prevent credit card usage for emergencies.

~SIXTEEN: Generosity and Safety Nets~

I learned one of the most counterintuitive lessons about money not from a financial advisor or business school professor, but from watching my neighbor Sarah navigate the 2008 financial crisis. While everyone else in our neighborhood was tightening their belts and cutting back, Sarah did something that seemed completely backward: she started giving more.

Sarah had been running a small catering business for three years when the economy crashed. Orders dried up almost overnight. Most entrepreneurs would have panicked, cut expenses, and hoarded every dollar. Instead, Sarah made a decision that would fundamentally change how I understood wealth. She offered free cooking classes to unemployed neighbors, donated leftover ingredients to the food bank, and created an informal meal-sharing network where families could trade home-cooked dishes.

What happened next defied every conventional wisdom about money management I'd ever learned. Within six months, Sarah's business had not only recovered but was thriving beyond its pre-crisis levels. The people she'd helped became her most loyal customers. The cooking classes led to new catering contracts. The meal-sharing network evolved into a community-supported agriculture program that generated steady revenue. Sarah had discovered what researchers now call the "generosity paradox": giving money away often leads to making more of it.

This wasn't luck or coincidence. Sarah had stumbled upon one of the most powerful principles of sustainable wealth building, one that completely transforms our relationship with financial security. When we shift from hoarding resources to creating value for others, we don't just build businesses—we build the kind of community safety nets that make true financial resilience possible.

Dr. Elizabeth Dunn's research at the University of British Columbia, published in *Science* journal in 2008, has consistently shown that people who spend money on others report greater happiness and life satisfaction than those who spend equivalent amounts on themselves. But the implications go far beyond feeling good. Her studies, documented in her 2013 book *Happy Money: The Science of Happier Spending*, reveal that generous individuals tend to earn more money over time, receive more promotions, and build stronger professional networks. The act of giving doesn't diminish our resources—it expands our capacity to create them.

I witnessed this principle in action during my years in the nuclear Navy. The sailors who consistently helped their shipmates with difficult technical problems weren't taken advantage of or left behind. They became the informal leaders others turned to for guidance. When promotion time came, these generous sailors had built reputations that opened doors. Their willingness to share knowledge hadn't depleted their own expertise—it had amplified their influence and created opportunities that benefited everyone involved.

The neuroscience behind this phenomenon is remarkable. When we engage in generous behavior, our brains release oxytocin, dopamine, and serotonin—chemicals that not only make us feel good but also improve our decision-making capabilities and stress resilience. Dr. Stephanie Brown's research at the University of Michigan, published in *Psychological Science* in 2003, found that older adults who provided help to others showed reduced mortality risk equivalent to that associated with exercising regularly. Generosity doesn't just create wealth; it creates the mental and physical health necessary to sustain wealth-building activities over time.

But perhaps most importantly, generous behavior changes how others perceive and interact with us. When we consistently create value for people without immediate expectation of return, we build what sociologists call "social capital"—a network of relationships characterized by trust, cooperation, and mutual support. This social capital becomes the foundation for business opportunities, career advancement, and financial security that no individual effort could achieve alone.

Understanding generosity as a wealth-creation strategy requires moving beyond random acts of kindness to strategic value creation. The most successful examples of generous wealth building share three common characteristics: they solve real problems, create scalable systems, and build community connections.

Consider the story of Muhammad Yunus, whose journey was documented in his 2007 book *Creating a World Without Poverty*. In 1976, Yunus was an economics professor in Bangladesh when he lent $27 of his own money to 42 women in a local village so they could purchase bamboo to make furniture. Traditional banks considered these women too risky to lend to, trapping them in cycles of poverty.

Yunus's simple act of trust launched what became the Grameen Bank, which has provided microloans to over 10 million borrowers worldwide, with a repayment rate exceeding 95% according to the bank's 2020 annual report. His "generous" decision to risk his own money on people others wouldn't trust didn't just help those women—it created a Nobel Prize-winning innovation that revolutionized global finance. The key insight was recognizing that what looked like charity was actually sound business based on understanding human nature and community dynamics.

The same principle operates at smaller scales in countless businesses and communities. When

Howard Schultz built Starbucks, he insisted on providing health insurance and stock options to part-time employees—benefits that were virtually unheard of in the retail industry. His approach was detailed in his 1997 book *Pour Your Heart Into It*. Critics called it financially reckless. Shareholders worried about the costs. But Schultz understood that generous treatment of employees would create the kind of customer experience that builds sustainable competitive advantage.

The results proved him right. Starbucks employees, who Schultz called "partners," provided consistently better customer service than competitors. Employee turnover dropped dramatically, reducing training costs and maintaining service quality. Customer loyalty increased, and the company's growth trajectory far exceeded industry norms. Research by the Harvard Business Review in 2003 showed that Starbucks' employee retention rate was 120% higher than the industry average. Schultz's "generous" employee policies weren't charity—they were strategic investments in human capital that generated extraordinary returns.

These examples reveal the key to strategic generosity: identifying opportunities where creating value for others simultaneously creates value for yourself. This isn't exploitation or manipulation. It's recognizing that the most sustainable forms of wealth creation occur when everyone benefits from the exchange.

One of the most profound discoveries in my journey toward financial resilience was realizing that individual wealth building, no matter how sophisticated, remains vulnerable without community support systems. The families and individuals who weather financial storms most effectively aren't necessarily those with the highest incomes—they're those embedded in networks of mutual support and reciprocal assistance.

I learned this lesson watching how different families in my childhood neighborhood responded to my father's periods of unemployment. Some neighbors operated from scarcity thinking, viewing any request for help as a threat to their own security. But others understood that helping neighbors in crisis was actually an investment in community stability that would benefit everyone long-term.

The families who practiced mutual aid created informal insurance systems more effective than anything available through traditional financial institutions. When the Johnsons needed help with childcare during a medical emergency, three neighbors stepped in immediately. When the Patels lost income due to company downsizing, their network helped with groceries and job referrals until they recovered. When the Martinez family faced unexpected car repairs that threatened their ability to get to work, community members pooled resources for the fix.

These weren't charity cases—they were reciprocal relationships where everyone contributed according to their ability and received support according to their need. The families involved in these networks experienced greater financial stability than neighbors with higher incomes but weaker community connections. They had created what economists call "social insurance"—community-based systems that provide security through shared risk rather than individual accumulation.

Modern research confirms what these families understood intuitively. Dr. Matthew Salganik's studies at Princeton University, published in the *American Journal of Sociology* in 2010, show that individuals embedded in strong social networks weather financial shocks better than those relying solely on personal savings. The key factor isn't the amount of money available, but the speed and reliability of support when crisis hits. Community safety nets provide what no individual preparation can: immediate response capacity and emotional support during high-stress situations.

Building these networks requires moving beyond transactional thinking to relationship building. The most effective community safety nets emerge when people consistently contribute small amounts of time, energy, or resources to mutual benefit projects. This might involve organizing neighborhood tool libraries, participating in skill-sharing groups, contributing to community gardens, or simply maintaining regular communication with neighbors about needs and resources.

The technology age has created new opportunities for community safety net development. Apps like Nextdoor, Buy Nothing groups on Facebook (launched in 2013), and local community networks enable resource sharing and mutual aid coordination at scales previously impossible. But the fundamental principle remains unchanged: communities that practice systematic generosity and mutual support create financial resilience that transcends individual circumstances.

The most powerful aspect of building wealth through generosity lies in understanding how generous systems create compound effects that benefit everyone involved. Unlike zero-sum thinking, where one person's gain requires another's loss, generous systems generate increasing returns that expand opportunities for all participants.

I experienced this firsthand when I started mentoring young professionals in my field. My initial motivation was simple: I remembered how valuable mentorship had been during my naval training and wanted to pay that forward. But what I discovered was that mentoring others dramatically accelerated my own professional development in ways I never anticipated.

Teaching complex concepts to newcomers forced me to deepen my own understanding. Answering their questions revealed gaps in my knowledge that I addressed through additional study. Helping them navigate career challenges kept me current with industry trends and emerging opportunities. Most surprisingly, several mentees eventually became valuable professional connections who brought opportunities my way years later.

This pattern—where helping others develop simultaneously develops yourself—appears consistently in research on professional networks and career advancement. Dr. Adam Grant's studies at Wharton, detailed in his 2013 book *Give and Take*, demonstrate that "givers" who consistently help others without immediate expectation of return tend to outperform both "takers" and "matchers" in long-term career success and financial outcomes.

The key insight is that generous behavior creates what systems theorists call "positive feedback loops." Each act of value creation for others enhances your reputation, skills, and network, which increases your capacity to create even more value in the future. Over time, these compounding effects generate opportunities and resources that far exceed what individual effort could achieve.

Consider how this principle operates in business contexts. Companies that consistently create exceptional value for customers don't just build sales—they build customer loyalty that reduces marketing costs and creates word-of-mouth referrals. A study by Bain & Company published in the *Harvard Business Review* in 2001 found that increasing customer retention rates by 5% increases profits by 25% to 95%. Organizations that invest generously in employee development don't just improve current performance—they build reputations that attract top talent and reduce recruitment costs. Entrepreneurs who freely share knowledge and resources don't just build goodwill—they create ecosystems of mutual support that generate business opportunities.

The compound effect extends beyond individual benefits to transform entire communities. When generous systems reach critical mass, they create what Robert Putnam documented in his 2000 book *Bowling Alone* as "social capital" that benefits everyone involved. Crime rates decrease, property values increase, local businesses thrive, and community resilience improves. The initial acts of generosity multiply through the network, creating value that returns to the original givers in forms they never could have planned or predicted.

The shift from hoarding to strategic generosity requires understanding how this transformation changes our fundamental relationship with money and security. When we operate from scarcity thinking, every dollar spent represents a loss of safety. When we understand abundance creation, every dollar invested in value creation represents a multiplication of possibilities.

This psychological transformation happened gradually for me, but one moment stands out as particularly significant. I was consulting with a small business owner who was struggling with cash flow. His instinct was to cut every possible expense and delay payments to vendors as long as possible. Instead, I suggested he implement a customer appreciation program that would require additional short-term investment but might generate long-term loyalty.

His initial reaction was visceral fear. How could spending more money solve a money problem? But after we analyzed successful examples and calculated potential returns, he agreed to try a limited pilot program. Within three months, customer retention had improved significantly, referrals were increasing, and cash flow was stabilizing. More importantly, his entire attitude toward money had shifted from defensive to creative.

This transformation from defensive money management to creative value generation represents one of the most important shifts in developing financial resilience. When we're focused on protecting what we have, we limit our ability to create more. When we're focused on creating value for others, we expand our capacity to generate resources in ways we never could have imagined.

Dr. Carol Dweck's research on growth mindset, published in her 2006 book *Mindset*, provides the psychological framework for understanding this shift. People with fixed mindsets view money as a finite resource that must be carefully guarded. People with growth mindsets view money as a tool for creating value that expands through use. This difference in perspective leads to completely different financial behaviors and dramatically different long-term outcomes.

The practical implications are profound. Instead of asking "How can I protect my money?" the question becomes "How can I create value that generates sustainable returns?" Instead of viewing generosity as a luxury available only after achieving security, generosity becomes a strategy for building security through community connection and value creation.

This doesn't mean abandoning prudent financial management or giving away money recklessly. It means recognizing that the most sustainable forms of financial security come from building systems that create value for others while generating returns for yourself. The goal isn't charitable giving—it's strategic value creation that benefits everyone involved.

The transformation from hoarding to strategic generosity creates the psychological foundation necessary for sustainable high performance. When we're constantly worried about financial security or focused on protecting what we have, our mental energy remains trapped in defensive mode. When we understand how to create security through value generation, we free our minds to focus on higher-level contributions.

This connection became clear to me during my transition from military service to civilian career. The nuclear Navy had provided comprehensive security—guaranteed income, housing, healthcare, and career progression. Leaving that system initially created anxiety about financial uncertainty. My first impulse was to find the safest possible job with the most secure benefits, even if it limited growth opportunities.

But applying the lessons of strategic generosity changed my approach entirely. Instead of seeking the most secure position, I looked for opportunities to create the most value. Instead of focusing on what I could get from employers, I focused on what I could contribute to their success. This shift in perspective led to opportunities I never would have discovered through defensive job hunting.

The psychological research supports this connection between financial security and cognitive performance. Dr. Sendhil Mullainathan's studies on scarcity psychology, detailed in his 2013 book *Scarcity*, show that financial stress literally reduces mental bandwidth available for complex problem-solving and creative thinking. When our minds are occupied with survival concerns, we lose access to the higher-order thinking capabilities necessary for innovation and productivity mastery.

Conversely, when we understand how to create financial security through value generation, we develop what psychologists call "approach motivation" rather than "avoidance motivation." We become focused on opportunities rather than threats, possibilities rather than problems. This mental shift is essential for developing the flow states and deep focus capabilities that characterize peak productivity.

The community safety nets built through generous systems provide another crucial element: the psychological security that comes from knowing we're not facing challenges alone. When we have strong relationships with people who understand our values and want to see us succeed, we're more willing to take the intelligent risks necessary for growth and innovation.

Actionable Steps:

How to implement: Start by creating a "value inventory" this week. List three skills or resources you have that could help others. Choose one person in your network who could benefit from these resources and offer help without expecting anything in return. Track how this generous action affects your relationship and any unexpected opportunities that emerge. Begin with 2 hours per month dedicated to helping others in your field or community.

When to do it: Schedule your first generous action within the next 7 days. Set a recurring monthly reminder to identify new opportunities for strategic generosity. The best time is when you feel financially stressed—counterintuitively, this is when generous actions provide the most psychological benefit and often lead to unexpected solutions.

Why this works: Neuroscience research shows that generous behavior releases oxytocin and serotonin, improving both mood and decision-making capability. Strategic generosity builds social capital that provides better returns than traditional networking. Studies show that people who regularly help others earn 5-10% more over their careers due to enhanced reputation and expanded opportunities. The practice shifts your mindset from scarcity to abundance, enabling creative problem-solving that defensive thinking blocks.

~SEVENTEEN: Finding Flow States~

Haruki Murakami sits down to write, and something magical happens. No phone notifications. No email checks. No social media scrolling. Just sustained focus that produces masterpieces like Norwegian Wood and The Wind-Up Bird Chronicle. Then, as if completing a sacred ritual, he runs ten kilometers or swims fifteen hundred meters, entering what he calls a "rhythmic movement trance" that somehow unlocks even deeper creative insights.

This isn't the romantic image of the tortured artist waiting for inspiration to strike. This is something far more powerful: the deliberate cultivation of flow states through systematic routine. As Murakami explains in his memoir "What I Talk About When I Talk About Running" (Alfred A. Knopf, 2008), he discovered what neuroscientists are only now beginning to understand—that peak performance isn't a mysterious gift reserved for the chosen few, but a predictable neurochemical state that can be triggered through specific environmental and behavioral cues.

I learned this lesson the hard way during my nuclear training in the Navy. Operating a nuclear reactor requires sustained attention for hours at a time—a single moment of distraction could be catastrophic. But I noticed something interesting about the technicians who excelled. They weren't necessarily the smartest or most technically gifted. They were the ones who could reliably enter what we now call flow states during critical operations. They had developed the ability to merge consciousness with action, to become so absorbed in the task that self-consciousness disappeared and performance became effortless.

Flow states represent one of the most fascinating discoveries in modern neuroscience. When researchers use brain imaging technology to study people in flow, they discover something remarkable: certain areas of the brain actually slow down. This phenomenon, called transient hypofrontality, involves the temporary downregulation of the prefrontal cortex—the part of your brain responsible for self-criticism, time awareness, and conscious control. As Dr. Arne Dietrich documented in his research published in Consciousness and Cognition (2003), this neural shift creates the conditions for optimal performance.

Think about the last time you were completely absorbed in an activity. Maybe you were having an engaging conversation, working on a challenging puzzle, or playing a sport you loved. Hours passed in what felt like minutes. Your inner critic went silent. You weren't worrying about how you looked or whether you were doing it "right"—you were simply doing it. This isn't just a pleasant psychological state; it's a measurable neurochemical shift that optimizes your brain for peak performance.

During flow, your brain releases a cocktail of performance-enhancing neurochemicals. Norepinephrine increases focus and attention. Dopamine heightens motivation and reward-seeking behavior. Endorphins block pain and create pleasure. Anandamide promotes lateral thinking and creative insights. This neurochemical symphony doesn't happen by accident—it emerges when specific conditions are met, as psychologist Mihaly Csikszentmihalyi first documented in his groundbreaking book "Flow: The Psychology of Optimal Experience" (Harper & Row, 1990).

The research reveals that flow states occur when challenge and skill are perfectly balanced. If the challenge is too high relative to your skill level, anxiety emerges. If the challenge is too low, boredom sets in. But in that sweet spot where challenge slightly exceeds skill, your nervous system clicks into a state of effortless concentration. Steven Kotler and the researchers at the Flow Research Collective have expanded on this work, showing through studies published in the Journal of Business Venturing (2020) that entrepreneurs who regularly access flow states are five times more productive than those who don't.

What makes Murakami extraordinary isn't just his literary talent—it's his systematic approach to creating conditions for sustained flow. His routine demonstrates critical principles that anyone can apply to their own work. By starting at the same time every day, his nervous system learns to anticipate and prepare for focused work. Sleep researchers like Dr. Matthew Walker, whose work is detailed in "Why We Sleep" (Scribner, 2017), have discovered that our circadian rhythms can be trained to optimize cognitive function at specific times. Some people naturally focus best in the morning, others find their peak performance in the afternoon or evening. The key isn't the specific time—it's the consistency of that chosen time.

Murakami's writing space is designed to minimize distraction and maximize focus. No internet connection. No phone access. Just the essential tools needed for writing. This isn't about being antisocial or disconnected—it's about recognizing that our modern environment is deliberately designed to fragment attention. Creating a sanctuary for deep work isn't luxury; it's necessity. Research published in the Journal of Environmental Psychology (2019) by Dr. Sally Augustin and colleagues shows that physical environment directly impacts cognitive performance and flow state access.

The integration of physical and mental practice sets Murakami's approach apart. The running or swimming isn't separate from his writing—it's part of the same system. The cardiovascular exercise increases brain-derived neurotrophic factor (BDNF), which promotes the growth of new neural connections, as documented in research published in Cell Metabolism (2013) by Dr. Christiane Wrann and colleagues. The rhythmic nature of endurance exercise also triggers a meditative state that researchers call "soft fascination"—a relaxed attention that allows the default mode network in your brain to make novel connections.

Murakami doesn't try to write for twelve hours straight. He works with focused intensity for five to six hours, then transitions to physical activity, then allows time for rest and recovery. This isn't because he lacks dedication—it's because he understands that flow states require both engagement and restoration. Research published in the Academy of Management Journal (2017) by Dr. Emily Hunter and Cindy Wu shows that without adequate recovery, our capacity for sustained flow diminishes rapidly.

I experienced a version of this during my nuclear training when I discovered that my best study sessions happened when I combined three elements: consistent timing, distraction-free environment, and regular movement breaks. The most complex reactor systems became comprehensible when I studied them in flow states rather than grinding through them with willpower alone. The training inadvertently taught me what researchers would later confirm: flow states can be systematically cultivated through environmental and behavioral design.

Physical environment design starts with understanding that your surroundings constantly communicate with your nervous system. Cluttered spaces signal chaos to your brain, while organized spaces signal order and control. Natural light enhances alertness and mood. Cool temperatures improve cognitive function. Minimizing visual distractions allows your brain to allocate more resources to the task at hand. Research by Dr. Craig Knight at the University of Exeter, published in the Journal of Experimental Psychology (2010), demonstrates that environmental control significantly impacts both productivity and psychological comfort.

Temporal boundaries prove equally important. Finding your optimal time for deep work isn't about following someone else's schedule—it's about discovering when your brain naturally peaks. The key is consistency. Your nervous system learns to anticipate and prepare for peak performance when you honor the same schedule day after day. Studies published in Trends in Cognitive Sciences (2018) by Dr. Russell Foster show that aligning work with circadian rhythms can improve performance by up to 30%.

Psychological boundaries require protecting your flow time from interruptions, requests, and the constant pull of reactive tasks. It means having difficult conversations with colleagues about when you're available and when you're not. It means turning off notifications and creating systems that allow you to be unreachable during your most important work. Research by Dr. Gloria Mark at UC Irvine, published in CHI Conference Proceedings

(2008), found that it takes an average of 23 minutes to fully refocus after an interruption.

Understanding how to calibrate challenge and skill becomes the difference between frustration and flow. Maya Lin's experience designing the Vietnam Veterans Memorial provides a powerful example. When she submitted her design as a 21-year-old Yale undergraduate, she was entering a competition against seasoned professionals. The challenge was immense, but her skills were precisely calibrated to meet it. She had studied architecture intensively, understood the memorial's purpose deeply, and possessed the creative vision to see what others couldn't. As documented in her book "Boundaries" (Simon & Schuster, 2000), the result was a design that emerged from a flow state—intuitive, powerful, and seemingly effortless.

This challenge-skill balance explains why many people struggle to access flow states in their daily work. If your job consistently presents challenges below your skill level, you experience boredom and disengagement. If the challenges consistently exceed your skills, you experience anxiety and overwhelm. But when you can adjust either the challenge level or develop your skills to create that sweet spot, flow becomes accessible. Research by Dr. Jeanne Nakamura, published in the Journal of Happiness Studies (2011), confirms that people who actively manage this balance report significantly higher life satisfaction.

What makes Murakami's approach particularly brilliant is his integration of physical movement with mental performance. The running and swimming aren't separate from his writing practice—they're part of the same flow system. This connection between movement and flow appears consistently across high performers in every field. Professional athletes during competition demonstrate this perfectly. A basketball player sinking shot after shot isn't thinking about mechanics or outcome—they're in a flow state where movement becomes effortless and time seems to slow down.

Research from the Flow Research Collective, published in Psychology of Sport and Exercise (2019), shows that people who engage in regular rhythmic movement—whether it's running, swimming, cycling, or even walking—report significantly higher levels of creativity and problem-solving ability. The repetitive, meditative nature of these activities triggers the same relaxed attention that characterizes flow states.

I discovered this connection during my nuclear training when I found that my most challenging study sessions became manageable after a swim or run. The physical activity didn't tire me out—it tuned me in. My brain operated more efficiently, complex concepts became clearer, and I could sustain focus for longer periods. The movement served multiple functions: providing a natural reset between focused work sessions, triggering the release of BDNF, and activating the same neurochemical pathways that characterize flow states.

Building reliable access to flow states requires developing a systematic approach tailored to your unique circumstances, energy patterns, and work demands. The goal isn't to copy someone else's routine but to understand the underlying principles and adapt them to your life. Neuroscientist Dr. Adam Gazzaley's research on cognitive training, published in Nature (2013), demonstrates that personalized approaches to flow cultivation are significantly more effective than one-size-fits-all methods.

The compound effect of regular flow state access transforms occasional peak experiences into sustained high performance. Each time you successfully enter a flow state, you're not just accomplishing the immediate task—you're strengthening the neural pathways that make future flow states more accessible. Think of flow cultivation like physical fitness. The first time you run, it's difficult and uncomfortable. But with consistent practice, your cardiovascular system adapts, your muscles strengthen, and what once felt impossible becomes routine.

Research from Dr. Arne Dietrich at American University of Beirut, published in Neuroscience & Biobehavioral Reviews (2004), shows that people who regularly experience flow states develop what he calls "transient hypofrontality on demand"—the ability to deliberately quiet the self-critical, time-conscious parts of their brain when focused performance is needed. This isn't just a psychological skill; it's a measurable neurological adaptation.

The long-term benefits extend beyond individual performance to overall life satisfaction. A longitudinal study published in the Journal of Personality (2018) by Dr. Teresa Freire and colleagues found that people who regularly experience flow states report higher levels of life satisfaction, better relationships, and greater resilience in the face of challenges. When you know you can reliably access your best self, you approach obstacles with confidence rather than anxiety.

The transformation from sporadic inspiration to reliable flow access requires patience and systematic practice. The journey begins with environment design—creating spaces and times that support sustained focus. Add movement integration next, finding ways to incorporate rhythmic physical activity that enhances rather than depletes your mental energy. Experiment with different challenge-skill balances, noting what level of difficulty produces engagement versus anxiety in your chosen domain.

Track your results not just in terms of output, but in terms of experience. How does your work feel when you're in flow versus when you're grinding through it with willpower alone? What conditions make flow more or less likely? What patterns emerge over time? The data you gather becomes invaluable for refining your approach and making flow states increasingly accessible.

Flow states represent the foundation upon which all other productivity improvements rest. When you can reliably access states of effortless concentration, systems can be optimized because you have the sustained attention to design them properly. Goals can be achieved because you can access the focused energy needed for consistent progress. Deep work becomes natural because you've learned to create the conditions that make it inevitable.

The science is clear: in a world of constant distraction, the ability to access flow states becomes an almost unfair competitive advantage. But more importantly, it represents a return to what human consciousness does best—complete absorption in meaningful challenges that stretch our capabilities while engaging our deepest interests. When we learn to cultivate these states systematically, we don't just become more productive. We become more fully alive to the possibilities each moment presents.

Actionable Steps:

How to implement: Start by identifying your natural energy rhythms through a two-week tracking period. Note your alertness and focus levels hourly from waking to sleeping. Once you identify your peak performance window (typically a 2-4 hour period), block this time for your most challenging work. Create a dedicated workspace free from digital distractions—remove or silence all devices, close unnecessary browser tabs, and use physical barriers if needed. Begin each flow session with a consistent 5-minute ritual (deep breathing, reviewing objectives, or light stretching) that signals to your nervous system it's time to focus. Start with 25-minute focused work blocks, gradually extending to 90 minutes as your flow capacity develops.

When to do it: Schedule your flow sessions during your identified peak energy window, maintaining the same time daily for at least 30 days to establish neural patterns. Plan movement breaks every 90 minutes—even a 5-minute walk resets attention. Integrate longer movement sessions (30-45 minutes of running, swimming, or cycling) either before your flow work to prime your nervous system or after to consolidate learning. Review and adjust your approach weekly based on what produces the most consistent flow access.

Why this works: Consistent timing trains your circadian rhythms to optimize neurotransmitter production for focus. Environmental control eliminates attention residue from competing stimuli, allowing full cognitive resources to engage with your chosen task. The challenge-skill balance triggers the neurochemical cascade of flow by creating enough difficulty to demand full attention without overwhelming your current capabilities. Regular movement increases BDNF production, enhances neuroplasticity, and provides the physical foundation for sustained mental performance. The compound effect of daily practice literally rewires your brain for easier flow access, creating a positive feedback loop where success breeds greater success.

~EIGHTEEN: Systems Over Goals~

My office wall was covered with goals. Annual revenue targets. Quarterly milestones. Monthly fitness objectives. Daily task lists color-coded by priority. I had downloaded every goal-tracking app, purchased every planner system, and attended seminars on SMART goal methodology. The irony was that despite this elaborate goal infrastructure, I felt like I was constantly falling short. Each unchecked box felt like a personal failure. Each missed target became evidence that I wasn't disciplined enough, focused enough, or committed enough.

The breakthrough came from studying a comedian's approach to productivity. Jerry Seinfeld, despite decades of consistent output and creative success, doesn't focus on writing brilliant jokes or achieving specific performance metrics. Instead, he follows a deceptively simple system that he shared with software developer Brad Isaac, as documented in Isaac's widely circulated blog post from 2007. Seinfeld's method revolves around a large wall calendar and a red marker. His only commitment is to write comedy material every day and mark an X on the calendar. After several days, a chain of X's forms. The entire system boils down to one rule: don't break the chain.

When I first encountered this approach through Gretchen Rubin's "Better Than Before" (2015), I dismissed it as too simplistic for serious productivity. Surely someone of Seinfeld's caliber had more sophisticated methods for maintaining creative output. But as I researched high performers across different fields, I discovered that the most successful people often rely on simple systems rather than complex goal frameworks.

The calendar method fundamentally shifts focus from outcomes to process. Traditional goal-setting asks, "What do I want to achieve?" The system approach asks, "What do I want to do consistently?" This distinction might seem semantic, but it creates profoundly different psychological experiences. Goals exist in the future and invite judgment about whether you've succeeded or failed. Systems exist in the present and simply require showing up.

I decided to test this approach with exercise, an area where I had repeatedly failed with traditional goal-setting. Instead of setting targets to lose specific amounts of weight or achieve certain fitness benchmarks, I created a simple system: do some form of physical movement every day and mark it on a calendar. The movement could be as minimal as five minutes of stretching or as intensive as a two-hour workout. The only requirement was daily action and marking the X.

The psychological shift was immediate. On busy days, instead of skipping exercise entirely because I couldn't do my "ideal" workout, I did ten pushups and marked my X. On energetic days, I naturally did more without feeling pressured by specific targets. The daily decision of whether to exercise disappeared. The system had already made that choice for me.

Stanford behavioral scientist BJ Fogg's research, published in his 2019 book "Tiny Habits," provides the scientific foundation for why this approach works. Fogg's studies at the Stanford Behavior Design Lab demonstrate that consistency matters more than intensity for creating lasting behavior change. When we perform small behaviors consistently, we strengthen neural pathways that make future performance increasingly automatic. Each repetition requires less conscious effort, eventually transforming deliberate practice into effortless habit.

The psychological advantages of systems over goals became even clearer as I expanded the approach to other areas. Goals create what psychologists call "arrival fallacy"—the mistaken belief that achieving a specific outcome will bring lasting satisfaction. Research by Dr. Tal Ben-Shahar at Harvard, documented in his 2007 book "Happier," shows that people often experience emptiness rather than fulfillment upon reaching major goals because the anticipation provided more satisfaction than the achievement itself.

Systems sidestep this problem entirely. When your commitment is to the process rather than the outcome, every day you honor the system is a day you succeed. There's no distant finish line to reach, no binary success or failure. Just the simple question: Did I do what I committed to doing today?

The compound effect of systematic action reveals itself over time in ways that goal-focused thinking often misses. Consider the difference between these two approaches to writing. Goal: "Write a novel this year." System: "Write for 30 minutes every day." The goal creates pressure and invites procrastination—after all, you have a whole year to complete it. The system creates momentum—after just one month, you've written for 15 hours, likely producing 15,000-20,000 words without the stress of tracking toward a specific target.

Research from the European Journal of Social Psychology (2010) by Dr. Phillippa Lally and colleagues found that habit formation takes an average of 66 days of consistent repetition. But this assumes daily practice. Sporadic efforts, regardless of intensity, rarely create lasting neural changes. The calendar method's visual tracking ensures the consistency that neuroscience shows is essential for behavioral change.

The genius of Seinfeld's approach extends beyond personal productivity to understanding the nature of creativity itself. Conventional wisdom suggests that creative work requires inspiration, that we should wait for the muse to strike. But Seinfeld's decades of consistent output demonstrate that creativity emerges from practice, not patience. By writing every day, he creates exponentially more opportunities for excellent material to emerge than someone waiting for perfect conditions.

I applied this insight to my own creative work. Instead of setting goals to complete specific projects or achieve certain quality standards, I established simple creative systems. Write for 30 minutes daily. Read for 20 minutes daily. Practice skill development for 15 minutes daily. The specific outputs varied dramatically—some days produced garbage, others generated breakthroughs—but the system ensured consistent forward movement.

The calendar method also addresses what behavioral economists Daniel Kahneman and Amos Tversky identified as loss aversion in their groundbreaking research published in Econometrica (1979). Humans feel losses approximately twice as intensely as equivalent gains. The visual chain of X's leverages this psychological tendency productively. Breaking the chain feels like losing something concrete and valuable, while skipping progress toward an abstract goal feels less immediately painful.

This insight revolutionized how I approached financial habits. Rather than setting savings goals with specific dollar amounts, I created a system:

transfer money to savings every payday and track it on a calendar. The amount could vary based on circumstances, but the transfer had to happen. This removed the emotional negotiation around saving and made it as automatic as any other system.

The research on implementation intentions by psychologist Peter Gollwitzer, published in the American Psychologist (1999), explains why systems outperform goals in behavior change. When we create specific if-then patterns (If it's Tuesday morning, then I write for 30 minutes), we offload decision-making from our conscious mind to environmental cues. This preserves willpower for truly important decisions rather than depleting it on routine choices.

Financial advisor and author David Bach describes a similar approach in "The Automatic Millionaire" (2003) with his "pay yourself first" system. Rather than setting goals to save specific amounts, he advocates automating transfers that happen before you have a chance to make decisions about the money. The system removes willpower from the equation entirely.

The productivity implications extend to organizations as well. James Clear, in "Atomic Habits" (2018), documents how British cycling transformed from mediocrity to dominance not through ambitious goals but through what performance director Dave Brailsford called "the aggregation of marginal gains." Instead of setting targets for race victories, they created systems for improving every component of cycling performance by 1%. The compound effect of these systematic improvements produced extraordinary results.

I experienced this organizational impact firsthand when implementing systems thinking in team management. Instead of setting quarterly targets that created stress and encouraged short-term thinking, we established daily and weekly rhythms that naturally produced better outcomes. Daily check-ins replaced quarterly reviews. Weekly retrospectives replaced annual performance evaluations. The consistency of these systems created more improvement than any goal-setting exercise ever had.

The most profound shift came when I realized that systems thinking transforms identity in ways that goal achievement cannot. When you set a goal to run a marathon, you're someone trying to become a runner. When you establish a system of daily movement, you become a runner through the accumulation of daily evidence. Each X on the calendar isn't just marking an action—it's reinforcing an identity.

Research by Dr. Anthony Grant at the University of Sydney, published in the International Coaching Psychology Review (2012), confirms this identity-based behavior change. People who focus on "being" rather than "achieving" show more sustainable behavior change and report higher life satisfaction. Systems naturally support identity development because they emphasize consistent action rather than distant outcomes.

The calendar method's simplicity also prevents what researchers call "complexity creep"—the tendency to make systems increasingly elaborate until they become unsustainable. I learned this lesson when I tried to track fifteen different daily habits simultaneously. The complexity of the tracking system became more burdensome than the habits themselves. Returning to simple calendar X's for 3-4 core practices proved far more effective than elaborate tracking schemes.

The fear many people express about systems thinking is that it might reduce ambition or discourage big dreams. The opposite proves true. When you're confident in your daily systems, you can pursue audacious long-term visions without the anxiety of wondering whether you'll follow through. The system handles the "how" so you can focus on the "why" and "what if."

Seinfeld's own career demonstrates this perfectly. He didn't set a goal to become one of the most successful comedians in history. He committed to writing jokes every day. The extraordinary success emerged from ordinary consistency, compounded over decades. The system didn't limit his ambitions—it made them achievable through sustainable daily practice.

As I integrated systems thinking more deeply into my life, I noticed how it reduced decision fatigue while increasing actual accomplishment. The mental energy previously spent on goal-setting, tracking, adjusting, and judging could be redirected toward execution and improvement. The systems handled the structure so I could focus on the substance.

The true power of systems over goals lies not in any single advantage but in how they transform our relationship with achievement itself. Goals make happiness conditional on future outcomes. Systems create satisfaction through present action. Goals invite comparison with others who might achieve more or faster. Systems focus on your own consistent progress. Goals create pressure that often paralyzes. Systems create momentum that naturally accelerates.

Actionable Steps:

Create a large wall calendar specifically for tracking your most important system. Physical visibility matters more than digital convenience. Place it where you'll see it multiple times daily—bathroom mirror, office wall, or kitchen. Buy a bold marker in your favorite color for marking X's.

Choose one behavior you want to systematize. Start with something you can do in under 10 minutes daily. Physical movement, writing, reading, or skill practice work well. The behavior should be specific enough to track but flexible enough to adapt to different circumstances.

Define your minimum viable action. What's the smallest version that still counts? For exercise, it might be 5 pushups. For writing, perhaps 50 words. For reading, maybe 1 page. This minimum ensures you can maintain the chain even on your worst days.

How to implement:

Begin immediately after reading this chapter. Don't wait for Monday, the first of the month, or the new year. Systems work because they start now, not at some perfect future moment. Mark your first X today, even if you need to retroactively do your minimum action.

Commit to 30 days before evaluating. Research shows it takes at least 21-66 days for neural pathways to solidify. Don't judge the system's effectiveness before giving it adequate time to create neurological changes. Focus solely on not breaking the chain for one month.

Track only completion, not quality or quantity. The calendar gets an X if you did the minimum action, period. Don't create gradations or partial credit. This binary tracking prevents perfectionism from sabotaging consistency.

When to do it:

Perform your systematic behavior at the same time each day when possible. Linking it to existing routines (after morning coffee, before lunch, after work) increases consistency through environmental cuing.

Mark your X immediately after completing the action. Don't wait until evening to mark multiple X's. The immediate visual reinforcement strengthens the neural reward pathway.

Review your chain weekly to appreciate your progress. Count the consecutive X's and notice how momentum builds. This reflection reinforces identity change—you're becoming someone who consistently does this behavior.

Why this works:

Systems eliminate decision fatigue by making action automatic rather than negotiated. You don't waste mental energy deciding whether to act today because the system already decided for you.

Visual progress tracking leverages loss aversion psychology. Once you have a chain of 10+ days, breaking it feels like genuine loss, motivating continuation more powerfully than pursuing abstract goals.

Daily minimums ensure sustainability. By keeping the bar low enough to clear on difficult days, you maintain momentum that naturally expands into larger efforts when energy permits.

Identity reinforcement through consistent action creates lasting change. Each X provides evidence that you're the type of person who does this behavior, eventually making it feel unnatural not to continue.

Systems thinking shifts focus from outcomes you can't control to actions you can control. This reduces anxiety while increasing actual progress, creating a positive feedback loop that sustains itself over time.

~NINETEEN: Deep Focus in a Distracted World~

The email notification broke my concentration for the third time in twenty minutes. I was attempting to analyze a complex financial model, work that required sustained mental effort, but my attention kept fracturing across multiple digital interruptions. Each time I returned to the spreadsheet, I had to reconstruct my mental model of the problem, losing precious cognitive momentum. By the end of the hour, I had made minimal progress despite feeling mentally exhausted.

This pattern of fragmented attention has become the defining challenge of modern work. We live in an era where billion-dollar companies employ teams of neuroscientists and behavioral psychologists to design products that capture and monetize our attention. The result is a crisis of focus that undermines our ability to engage in what computer science professor Cal Newport calls "deep work"—the cognitively demanding activities that create significant value and require sustained concentration.

Newport's research, detailed in his 2016 book "Deep Work: Rules for Focused Success in a Distracted World," reveals a paradox of our time. Just as the ability to focus deeply is becoming increasingly rare, it's also becoming increasingly valuable. The automation of routine tasks means that the remaining human work requires precisely the kind of sustained thinking that our digital environment makes difficult to achieve.

Newport himself embodies the principles he advocates. As a computer science professor at Georgetown University, he has published multiple peer-reviewed papers, written several books, and maintained a popular blog—all without ever having a social media account. His deliberate rejection of these platforms isn't based on technophobia but on a calculated assessment of their impact on cognitive performance. "The ability to perform deep work is becoming increasingly rare at exactly the same time it is becoming increasingly valuable in our economy," Newport writes. "As a consequence, the few who cultivate this skill, and then make it the core of their working life, will thrive."

The neuroscience supporting Newport's approach is compelling. Research published in the journal Nature Communications in 2016 by Dr. Adam Gazzaley and colleagues demonstrated that our brains cannot actually multitask in the way we imagine. Instead, we engage in rapid task-switching, with each switch carrying a cognitive cost. These "switching costs" may seem minimal in isolation—perhaps a few seconds to reorient our attention—but they compound throughout the day, significantly degrading our intellectual capacity.

More concerning is how constant task-switching literally rewires our brains. A 2015 study in the Journal of Experimental Psychology by Dr. Kep Kee Loh and Dr. Ryota Kanai found that people who frequently multitask show reduced gray matter density in the anterior cingulate cortex, a region associated with cognitive and emotional control. We're not just temporarily distracting ourselves; we're permanently altering our neural architecture in ways that make sustained focus more difficult.

Newport's solution centers on cultivating what he terms "deep work sessions"—extended periods of uninterrupted concentration on cognitively demanding tasks. His approach isn't about working more hours but about maximizing the cognitive value produced during the hours we do work. He structures his days around four-hour blocks of deep work, during which he disconnects entirely from internet access and focuses on a single important project.

This practice builds on research from K. Anders Ericsson, published in Psychological Review in 1993, which established that elite performers in fields ranging from music to athletics engage in what he called "deliberate practice"—focused, goal-oriented work sessions that push the boundaries of current ability. Ericsson found that even elite performers could sustain this level of concentration for only about four hours per day, suggesting a natural limit to our capacity for deep cognitive work.

I experienced the power of this approach firsthand when I began implementing Newport's strategies in my own work. The transformation didn't happen immediately. My first attempts at extended focus sessions were almost physically uncomfortable. After years of reflexively checking email and responding to notifications, sitting with a single task for hours felt unnatural, even anxiety-inducing.

The breakthrough came when I started treating focus like a skill to be systematically developed rather than a natural ability I should already possess. I began with shorter sessions—just 45 minutes of uninterrupted work—and gradually extended them as my concentration capacity improved. Within months, I could sustain three-hour deep work sessions that produced more valuable output than entire days of fragmented effort.

The environmental design principles Newport advocates proved crucial to this transformation. He recommends creating what he calls a "deep work sanctuary"—a physical space optimized for concentration. This doesn't require an elaborate home office. It simply means establishing clear boundaries between spaces for focused work and spaces for other activities. When I designated a specific corner of my home exclusively for deep work, my brain began associating that space with concentrated effort, making the transition into focus mode increasingly automatic.

Newport's approach extends beyond individual work sessions to encompass what he calls "attention capital theory." He argues that in a knowledge economy, an organization's output depends on the aggregate attention capital of its workers—their total capacity for deep, focused work. Companies that protect and cultivate this attention capital will outperform those that allow it to be fragmented by constant meetings, open office plans, and always-on communication expectations.

This theory finds support in research from the University of California, Irvine. Dr. Gloria Mark's studies, published in the CHI Conference proceedings in 2018, found that after an interruption, it takes an average of 23 minutes and

15 seconds to fully refocus on the original task. In a typical office environment where workers are interrupted every 11 minutes, this means many people never reach their full cognitive potential during an entire workday.

The implications extend far beyond individual productivity. Organizational psychologist Adam Grant, profiled in the New York Times Magazine in 2016, structures his work around similar principles. Grant batches his teaching responsibilities into concentrated periods, allowing for extended stretches of uninterrupted research and writing time. This approach has made him one of the most productive researchers in his field, with numerous publications in top-tier journals like the Academy of Management Journal and Psychological Science.

Grant's strategy of "batching" similar tasks reflects another key principle of deep work: minimizing context switching. When we group similar activities together—all our email in designated blocks, all our meetings on specific days—we reduce the cognitive overhead of constantly shifting between different types of work. This allows us to maintain what researchers call "cognitive momentum," the mental state where insights build upon each other naturally.

The challenge, of course, is implementing these principles in workplaces that seem designed to prevent deep focus. Open office plans, constant Slack notifications, and the expectation of immediate email responses create what Newport calls "the hyperconnected hive mind workflow"—a approach to work that prioritizes constant communication over concentrated effort.

Breaking free from this pattern requires what Newport terms "fixed-schedule productivity." Rather than working until all tasks are complete, he advocates defining clear work hours and then forcing all activities to fit within those boundaries. This constraint creates pressure to eliminate low-value activities and protect time for deep work. "Clarity about what matters provides clarity about what does not," Newport explains.

The science of attention restoration provides another crucial component of sustainable deep work practice. Research by Dr. Marc Berman and colleagues, published in Psychological Science in 2008, demonstrated that spending time in nature can restore directed attention capacity. This explains why many deep workers, including Newport, incorporate regular walks or outdoor activities into their routines. These aren't breaks from work but essential components of maintaining cognitive performance.

I discovered this connection between physical movement and mental focus during my own deep work experiments. A brief walk between focused sessions didn't just provide physical relief; it seemed to reset my cognitive capacity, allowing me to return to demanding tasks with renewed mental energy. This aligns with neuroscience research showing that light physical activity increases production of brain-derived neurotrophic factor (BDNF), which supports cognitive function and neural plasticity.

The role of boredom in developing deep work capacity surprised me. Newport argues that our constant stimulation-seeking behavior has atrophied our ability to tolerate boredom, which is actually a necessary precursor to deep focus. He recommends practices like "productive meditation"—using physically idle time like commuting or walking to work through professional problems without external input.

Research from the University of Central Lancashire, published in the Creativity Research Journal in 2013 by Dr. Sandi Mann and Dr. Rebekah Cadman, supports this counterintuitive approach. They found that people who engaged in a boring task before a creative challenge significantly outperformed those who moved directly to the creative work. Boredom, it seems, primes our brains for deeper engagement and more innovative thinking.

The digital minimalism philosophy Newport advocates extends beyond work hours. He argues for a comprehensive audit of our digital tools, keeping only those that provide substantial value toward our most important goals. This isn't about becoming a Luddite but about making intentional choices about which technologies deserve our attention.

This approach requires overcoming what Newport calls "the any-benefit mindset"—the tendency to adopt any tool or platform that provides any positive benefit, without considering the attention costs. A social media platform might occasionally surface interesting articles, but if it fragments our attention throughout the day, the net impact on our cognitive capacity could be severely negative.

The transformation from scattered attention to sustained focus doesn't happen overnight. It requires deliberate practice, environmental design, and often significant changes to established work patterns. But the payoff is substantial. In my own experience, developing deep work capacity didn't just improve my professional output—it enhanced my overall sense of control and satisfaction with life.

Research from Harvard psychologists Matthew Killingsworth and Daniel Gilbert, published in Science in 2010, found that people spend nearly half their waking hours thinking about something other than what they're currently doing, and this mind-wandering typically makes them unhappy. The capacity for sustained focus isn't just about productivity; it's about presence and engagement with our actual lives.

The compound effect of deep work practice extends beyond immediate productivity gains. As Newport notes, in a world where most knowledge workers struggle to focus for more than a few minutes at a time, those who can sustain concentration for hours possess an almost unfair advantage. They can master complex skills faster, produce higher-quality work, and tackle challenges that seem impossible to their perpetually distracted peers.

The future belongs not to those who can juggle the most tasks or respond to messages fastest, but to those who can think deeply about complex problems and create innovative solutions. In an economy increasingly dominated by artificial intelligence and automation, the uniquely human capacity for sustained creative thought becomes our most valuable asset. Protecting and cultivating this capacity isn't just a productivity strategy—it's an investment in our continued relevance and fulfillment in the digital age.

Actionable Steps:

How to implement: Begin by conducting a distraction audit for one week. Track every interruption during your workday, noting the source, duration, and impact on your focus. Use this data to identify your biggest attention drains. Then, create a dedicated deep work space—even if it's just a specific chair or corner of a room—that you use exclusively for focused work. Start with 45-minute deep work sessions with all notifications disabled and no internet access unless absolutely necessary for the task. Gradually increase session length by 15 minutes each week until you can sustain 2-3 hour blocks. Install website blockers like Freedom or

Cold Turkey during these sessions to eliminate temptation.

When to do it: Schedule your first deep work session for tomorrow during your natural peak energy time—for most people, this is within 2-4 hours of waking. Block this time on your calendar as a non-negotiable appointment. Conduct the distraction audit starting immediately and continuing for seven consecutive days. Set up your dedicated workspace today, even if it's simply clearing a table and putting a "Do Not Disturb" sign nearby. Begin with just one deep work session per day, ideally at the same time, to build the habit before adding additional sessions.

Why this works: The distraction audit creates awareness of how fragmented your current attention actually is—most people severely underestimate their interruption frequency. Dedicated space triggers environmental conditioning, where your brain learns to associate specific locations with focused work. Starting with shorter sessions prevents the overwhelm that causes people to abandon deep work practice, while gradual increases build your concentration capacity like training a muscle. Website blockers remove the need for willpower by making distraction physically impossible during work sessions. Scheduling sessions during peak energy times leverages your natural circadian rhythms for maximum cognitive performance, while consistency at the same time daily helps establish automatic behavioral patterns that require less conscious effort to maintain.

~TWENTY: Adaptive Productivity~

The rejection letter landed on my desk with the finality of a judge's gavel. Another investor had passed on my business proposal, the third in two weeks. I sat in my Atlanta hotel room, staring at the carefully crafted business plan that suddenly felt like nothing more than expensive paper filled with wishful thinking. My systematic approach to productivity, all those carefully plotted timelines and meticulously calculated projections, seemed to be working against me rather than for me.

That same week, I came across an article about Sara Blakely in Inc. Magazine (October 2012) that would fundamentally reshape my understanding of what productivity truly means. Blakely had started Spanx with $5,000 in savings and an idea born from cutting the feet off her pantyhose. But what struck me wasn't her innovative product idea—it was her approach to navigating the countless obstacles that followed.

When Blakely first attempted to sell her concept to hosiery manufacturers, she faced rejection after rejection. As she recounted in her interview with Forbes (March 2012), "I heard 'no' for two straight years. Most people thought I'd gone crazy." A rigid productivity mindset would have interpreted these rejections as clear signals to abandon the project and move on to something with better odds. Instead,

Blakely demonstrated what I now understand as adaptive productivity: the ability to maintain forward momentum while intelligently adjusting course based on new information.

After months of manufacturers refusing to even consider her idea, Blakely finally found success through an unexpected route. As she explained in "How I Built This" podcast with Guy Raz (September 2016), the breakthrough came when she called a manufacturer in North Carolina and the male owner initially dismissed her. But when she mentioned that his product would help women feel more confident, he asked his two daughters about it. They convinced him to give Blakely a chance. This wasn't part of any business plan—it was intelligent adaptation to circumstances.

The path forward proved anything but linear. The first prototypes came back wrong. The packaging she'd designed didn't work on store shelves. The patent attorney she consulted told her the idea wasn't protectable. Each setback required not just persistence, but the wisdom to adapt her approach while maintaining her core vision. As Blakely told Fortune Magazine (October 2013), "I had to be willing to pivot constantly while never losing sight of the problem I was trying to solve."

What fascinated me about Blakely's journey was how she balanced systematic effort with flexible execution. She maintained disciplined routines—cold-calling potential manufacturers every day, refining her pitch after each rejection, studying the hosiery market intensively. But she never let these systems become rigid constraints. When one approach failed, she quickly pivoted to another, treating each setback as valuable data rather than definitive defeat.

This revelation transformed how I thought about my own productivity systems. I had been so focused on creating perfect plans and executing them flawlessly that I'd forgotten the most crucial productivity skill: the ability to adapt intelligently when reality doesn't match your projections. The rejection letters on my desk weren't evidence that my plans were worthless—they were information about what needed to be adjusted.

The neuroscience behind adaptive productivity reveals why this flexibility is so essential. Research published in the Journal of Cognitive Neuroscience (2018) by Dr. Aron K. Barbey and colleagues at the University of Illinois shows that our brains function as prediction machines, constantly creating models of how the world works and what will happen next. This predictive capacity serves us well in stable environments, but it can become a liability when we cling too rigidly to mental models that no longer match reality.

Dr. Sian Beilock's research at the University of Chicago, published in Current Directions in Psychological Science (2008), demonstrates that cognitive flexibility—the ability to switch between different mental frameworks—is one of the strongest predictors of success in complex, changing environments. People who can maintain their core objectives while adapting their methods show consistently higher achievement across domains ranging from athletics to business to creative endeavors.

This doesn't mean abandoning the systematic thinking I'd developed through years of studying productivity masters. The key insight was learning to distinguish between principles that should remain constant and methods that should evolve with circumstances. I began thinking of this as "principled flexibility"—staying firmly committed to core values and objectives while remaining fluid about the specific tactics used to achieve them.

Professional athletes exemplify this balance beautifully. A tennis player might spend thousands of hours perfecting their serve through repetitive practice, building muscle memory and technical precision. But during an actual match, they must constantly adapt that serve based on their opponent's positioning, the wind conditions, the score, and their own fatigue level. The foundational technique remains constant, but the application varies with every point. The systematic practice creates the foundation, but adaptive execution wins matches.

Blakely demonstrated this same principle throughout Spanx's development. Her core principle—solving real undergarment problems for women—never wavered. But everything else evolved based on feedback and circumstances. When traditional department store buyers initially rejected Spanx, she didn't abandon retail distribution. Instead, she adapted her approach. As she recounted in her MasterClass (2020), she started personally demonstrating the product in department store bathrooms, showing potential customers the before-and-after effect. This guerrilla marketing tactic wasn't in any business school textbook, but it was a brilliant adaptation to the specific challenge she faced.

The breakthrough moment came when Oprah Winfrey named Spanx one of her "Favorite Things" in November 2000. But even this success required rapid adaptation. Blakely's systems weren't designed for the sudden surge in demand that followed Oprah's endorsement. As she told the New York Times (November 2011), "We went from shipping 3,000 units a month to needing to ship 20,000 units in three weeks." A rigid adherence to existing systems would have meant disappointing customers and squandering the opportunity. Instead, she rapidly reorganized her entire operation, bringing in temporary help, negotiating rush manufacturing, and completely redesigning her fulfillment process.

I began developing what I call "pivot protocols"—systematic ways to recognize when adaptation is needed and how to execute changes without losing momentum. Instead of viewing plan changes as failures, I started treating them as natural evolutions in any complex undertaking. This shift in perspective proved liberating. It allowed me to maintain the benefits of systematic thinking while avoiding the trap of inflexible adherence to plans that no longer served their purpose.

The first element of building adaptive productivity is creating better feedback loops. Most productivity systems excel at execution but neglect evaluation. They tell you how to complete tasks efficiently but don't help you assess whether those tasks are still moving you toward your actual goals. Adaptive productivity requires building in regular checkpoints where you honestly evaluate not just your progress, but the continued relevance of your chosen path.

I instituted weekly reviews where I asked three fundamental questions: What's working? What's not working? What needs to change? This wasn't about judging my performance against some predetermined standard, but about gathering real-time intelligence on the effectiveness of my current approach. Often, I discovered that I was efficiently executing tactics that had become disconnected from my strategic objectives—like a sailor making excellent time in the wrong direction.

Research by Harvard Business School professor Rita McGrath, published in Harvard Business Review (July 2013), reveals that successful entrepreneurs use what she calls "discovery-driven planning." Instead of creating detailed plans based on untested assumptions, they design small experiments that validate or invalidate their hypotheses before making major commitments. This approach maintains the rigor of systematic thinking while building in flexibility to adapt based on actual results rather than hopeful projections.

Netflix exemplifies this principle at an organizational level. As documented in "That Will Never Work" by co-founder Marc Randolph (2019), the company began by mailing DVDs to customers, a business model that seemed revolutionary at the time. But they didn't become attached to that specific method of content delivery. When streaming technology became viable, they pivoted their entire business model. When content licensing became expensive and restrictive, they pivoted again into original content production. Each transformation built on previous capabilities while adapting to new realities. The constant throughout was their core mission: making entertainment more convenient and accessible. Everything else—technology, business model, content strategy—remained negotiable.

Another crucial element of adaptive productivity is maintaining what researchers call "strategic reserves." This concept, borrowed from military strategy, means deliberately keeping some capacity available for unexpected opportunities or necessary pivots. It contradicts the common productivity advice to maximize efficiency by utilizing every available resource. Adaptive productivity recognizes that true effectiveness sometimes requires deliberate inefficiency in the short term to preserve flexibility for the long term.

Blakely exemplified this principle by keeping her day job selling fax machines for two years after starting Spanx. As she explained in Inc. Magazine (September 2014), this wasn't because she lacked confidence in her business idea. Rather, maintaining that financial stability gave her the freedom to make decisions based on long-term vision rather than short-term financial pressure. The "strategic reserve" of her steady salary allowed her to turn down unfavorable deals and wait for the right opportunities.

Learning to distinguish between productive adaptation and reactive panic became another essential skill. Not every obstacle requires a major pivot. Sometimes persistence through temporary challenges is exactly what's needed. The key is developing the judgment to recognize when you're facing a temporary setback versus when you're hitting a fundamental wall that requires a different approach.

Dr. Angela Duckworth's research on grit, published in Journal of Personality and Social Psychology (2007), provides useful guidance here. She found that successful individuals demonstrate both persistence in pursuing long-term goals and flexibility in their tactics. They're stubborn about their destination but flexible about their route. This nuanced understanding helps distinguish between giving up too easily and persisting with approaches that genuinely aren't working.

I learned this distinction painfully when I spent six months pursuing a marketing strategy that showed consistently poor results. My systematic mindset kept telling me to give the plan more time, to trust the process. But I had confused persistence with stubbornness, treating my refusal to adapt as a virtue rather than recognizing it as a blind spot. The adaptive mindset would have recognized much earlier that the fundamental assumptions underlying the strategy were flawed and required revision.

Building adaptive productivity also requires developing what psychologists call "tolerance for ambiguity"—the ability to function effectively in uncertain situations without rushing to premature closure. Dr. Stanley Budner's research at Columbia University, published in Journal of Personality (1962), showed that individuals with higher tolerance for ambiguity perform better in complex, changing environments because they can hold multiple possibilities in mind without becoming paralyzed by indecision.

This doesn't mean being wishy-washy or avoiding commitment. It means being strategic about where you make firm commitments and where you maintain flexibility. I learned to make irreversible decisions slowly and reversible decisions quickly, to commit firmly to principles while holding tactics lightly, to maintain clear direction while preserving multiple options for reaching the destination.

The practice of adaptive productivity also requires developing different modes of operation for different situations. Sometimes deep focus and systematic execution are exactly what's needed. Other times, exploration and experimentation are more valuable. The key is recognizing which mode fits the current challenge and being able to switch between them fluidly.

Dr. Barbara Oakley's research on learning, detailed in "A Mind for Numbers" (2014), describes this as the difference between "focused mode" and "diffuse mode" thinking. Both are essential, but they serve different purposes. Focused mode helps us execute known solutions efficiently. Diffuse mode helps us discover new solutions when existing approaches aren't working. Adaptive productivity requires mastery of both modes and the wisdom to know when each is appropriate.

This connects directly to the broader resilience themes woven throughout our journey. Physical resilience comes from building strength while maintaining flexibility—tight muscles might be strong, but they're also prone to injury. Mental resilience emerges from developing firm principles while remaining open to new information. Financial resilience requires building security while maintaining liquidity for opportunities. Productivity resilience follows the same pattern: building effective systems while preserving the ability to evolve them.

As I reflected on Blakely's journey from that initial $5,000 investment to building a billion-dollar company, I realized that her success came not from having a perfect plan, but from maintaining perfect adaptability. She combined the discipline to work systematically toward her vision with the flexibility to adjust her methods based on reality. This balance between structure and fluidity, between persistence and pivoting, represents the essence of adaptive productivity.

The transformation from rigid planning to adaptive execution opens possibilities that systematic thinking alone cannot access. It allows you to maintain momentum through uncertainty, capitalize on unexpected opportunities, and evolve your approach as you learn and grow. Most importantly, it prevents you from becoming trapped by your own systems, ensuring that your productivity methods serve your goals rather than constraining them.

Sara Blakely's story demonstrates that the highest form of productivity isn't about executing plans flawlessly—it's about maintaining forward progress while intelligently adapting to the ever-changing landscape of reality. When we develop this adaptive capacity, we don't just become more productive; we become antifragile, growing stronger through the very challenges that would break a more rigid approach. This is the kind of productivity that doesn't just achieve goals but evolves them, that doesn't just complete tasks but transforms them into stepping stones toward something even better than we originally imagined.

Actionable Steps:

How to implement: Start by creating a weekly review ritual every Sunday evening. Set aside 30 minutes to assess your current projects and goals using three questions: What's working? What's not working? What needs to change? Write your answers in a dedicated notebook. For each item that's not working, design a small experiment to test a different approach rather than abandoning the goal entirely. Track the results of these experiments over the following week.

When to do it: Schedule your weekly reviews for the same time each week, ideally Sunday evening when you can reflect on the past week and plan for the upcoming one. Implement pivot experiments immediately when you identify something that's not working. Don't wait for the "perfect" alternative—test small changes quickly and iterate based on results.

Why this works: Regular reviews prevent you from persisting with ineffective approaches due to sunk cost fallacy or misplaced loyalty to your original plan. The three-question framework forces honest assessment without harsh self-judgment. Small experiments reduce the risk of major pivots while providing real data about what works. This systematic approach to adaptation combines the benefits of structure with the necessity of flexibility, allowing you to maintain momentum while evolving your methods based on reality rather than assumptions.

~TWENTY-ONE: Creating Meaningful Rituals~

The productivity systems I had built were functioning with impressive efficiency. My calendar method generated consistent output, deep focus sessions produced breakthrough work, and adaptive frameworks handled unexpected changes smoothly. Yet beneath all this optimization, a fundamental question remained unanswered: What was the point of all this productivity?

The answer emerged through studying Viktor Frankl's revolutionary insights about human resilience. In his book "Man's Search for Meaning" (Beacon Press, 1959), Frankl documented observations from his time in Nazi concentration camps that would transform our understanding of what makes life worth living. While imprisoned at Auschwitz and other camps between 1942 and 1945, he noticed that survival wasn't determined by physical strength or favorable circumstances. Those who endured weren't necessarily the healthiest or most privileged—they were the ones who maintained meaning in their suffering.

Frankl's discovery was profound: while we cannot control what happens to us, we retain the power to choose our response. More significantly, we can construct meaning from any circumstance we face. This wasn't denial or wishful thinking—it was the deliberate creation of significance through ritual and practice.

I encountered Frankl's work during a period when all my carefully constructed systems felt hollow. The physical conditioning, mental training, financial security, and productivity mastery I had developed seemed impressive on paper but emotionally vacant. I had built an elaborate life optimization machine without clarifying what kind of life was worth optimizing.

Frankl developed what he termed logotherapy, based on the Greek word "logos" meaning purpose. His therapeutic approach rested on the premise that humans are primarily motivated not by pleasure (as Freud suggested) or power (as Adler claimed), but by the search for meaning. In the camps, Frankl observed that prisoners who maintained small rituals, found ways to serve others, or held onto future projects showed greater psychological resilience. They had transformed meaningless brutality into purposeful endurance.

The power of this approach became personal when my father died. The productivity systems that had served me well suddenly felt irrelevant against the randomness of grief. Tasks continued getting completed, but nothing felt significant. I was functioning without truly living.

The breakthrough came through studying how different cultures create meaning through ritual.

Research by Dr. Francesca Gino and Michael Norton, published in the Journal of Experimental Psychology (2013), reveals that ritual isn't mere ceremony—it's a technology for transforming unstructured experiences into meaningful patterns. When we create structured responses to life's chaos, we shift from being victims of circumstance to authors of significance.

I began developing personal meaning-making rituals, starting with how I honored my father's memory. Rather than letting grief ambush me randomly throughout each day, I created a specific practice. Every Sunday, I would read one page from a book he had recommended, then write a paragraph about how his values were manifesting in my current decisions. This simple ritual transformed scattered sorrow into structured reflection.

The neuroscience supporting this transformation is compelling. Research by Dr. Dimitrios Kapogiannis and colleagues, published in Brain Structure and Function (2009), shows that repeated, intentional practices connecting current experience to larger themes literally rewire our brains for meaning-making. The hippocampus begins linking present events to broader patterns while the prefrontal cortex automatically seeks significance rather than merely reacting to stimuli.

This explains why Frankl's approach succeeded even in extreme circumstances. By maintaining meaning-making rituals, survivors were training their brains to construct significance even when external conditions suggested only meaninglessness.

Building on this foundation, I developed what I call "purpose practices"—daily rituals specifically designed to connect immediate activities with deeper values. The insight is that meaning isn't discovered; it's created through consistent practice.

The first practice I developed was the "why before what" ritual. Before beginning any significant work session, I spend two minutes writing about why this work matters within my larger value system. Not productivity goals or external outcomes, but deeper significance. Why does this work serve something beyond myself? How does it connect to the person I aspire to become?

This simple ritual transformed my relationship with productivity entirely. Tasks stopped being obligations and became opportunities for value expression. The same focus sessions that previously felt like optimization exercises now felt like spiritual practice. I wasn't merely completing tasks; I was becoming someone through the doing.

The second practice emerged from research on grief recovery. Studies by Dr. George Bonanno at Columbia University, published in Clinical Psychology Review (2004), show that people who recover most fully from tragedy aren't those who "move on," but those who find ways to transform loss into service. They convert personal pain into purposeful action.

I created the "service connection" ritual. Each week's end, I identify one way my current work could serve someone beyond myself. Not in grandiose terms, but through specific, practical applications. How might the systems I'm building help others develop resilience? How can insights I'm gaining reduce someone else's suffering?

This practice connected personal optimization to something larger. Physical conditioning wasn't just about health—it demonstrated sustainable self-care for others. Mental resilience wasn't just about performance—it showed that ordinary people can develop extraordinary psychological strength. Financial security wasn't just about comfort—it created freedom to choose service over survival.

The third practice came from studying master craftspeople. Research by Dr. Mihaly Csikszentmihalyi, documented in "Flow: The Psychology of Optimal Experience" (Harper & Row, 1990), reveals how artisans maintain motivation across decades of skill development. They transform routine work into sacred practice through complete presence.

I developed the "presence pause" ritual. Between activity transitions, I take thirty seconds to appreciate the opportunity for full engagement with whatever comes next. Not gratitude as positive thinking, but genuine appreciation for bringing complete attention to meaningful work.

This practice revealed how much meaning I had been missing by rushing between tasks. When I slowed enough to recognize each activity as an opportunity for full engagement, even routine work became rich with significance. Email responses became chances to practice clear communication. Exercise became opportunities to honor physical capacity. Financial planning became expressions of values through resource allocation.

The fourth practice emerged from studying indigenous wisdom traditions. Research by Dr. Joseph P. Gone at Harvard University, published in Transcultural Psychiatry (2013), examines how indigenous cultures maintain ancestral wisdom through ritual practices. They transform historical knowledge into living wisdom through regular ceremony.

I created the "wisdom integration" ritual. Monthly, I select one insight from someone I respect—whether historical figures like Frankl, contemporary researchers, or personal mentors—and spend thirty days experimenting with how that insight influences current decisions. Not just intellectual understanding, but practical integration.

This practice connected my development to humanity's broader wisdom stream. Discipline became living practice rather than memory.

Emotional intelligence became daily choice rather than abstract knowledge. Systematic thinking became a framework for approaching all challenges.

Research by Dr. Crystal Park at the University of Connecticut, published in Psychological Bulletin (2010), confirms that meaning-making practices strengthen all areas of development. Physical conditioning becomes more sustainable when connected to values beyond appearance. Mental resilience becomes more accessible when serving something larger than comfort. Financial decisions clarify when expressing deeper principles. Productivity systems gain power when driving meaningful contribution.

The profound realization was that meaning isn't the result of achievement—it's the foundation making achievement worthwhile. When we build rituals consistently connecting daily activities to deeper values, every action becomes an expression of purpose.

These practices revealed what Frankl discovered in the camps: consistent meaning-creation makes us antifragile not just to external pressure but to internal emptiness. Research by Dr. Veronika Huta and Dr. Richard Ryan, published in Journal of Happiness Studies (2010), identifies this as "eudaimonic well-being"—deep satisfaction from living according to authentic values.

The neuroscience confirms Frankl's intuitive understanding. Studies by Dr. Adam Waytz and colleagues at Northwestern University, published in Journal of Experimental Social Psychology (2015), show that regular meaning-making practices strengthen neural networks responsible for purpose, connection, and transcendence. We literally train our brains to construct significance from life's raw material.

This explains ritual's power for resilience. It's not about specific ceremonies but training ourselves to transform experience into meaning through intentional response. Whether facing extreme adversity or everyday disappointments, the principle remains: we become who we are through what we repeatedly do with conscious intention.

The goal isn't eliminating suffering or guaranteeing positive outcomes. It's ensuring that whatever we experience serves meaningful development. When we build rituals connecting immediate experience to deeper purpose, we create what Frankl called "meaning-centered resilience"—the ability to find significance in any circumstance.

This foundation of meaningful ritual becomes essential for navigating life's deepest questions about authentic living and growth through adversity. When we've established practices for creating meaning, we're prepared to transform any experience into an opportunity for development serving something larger than ourselves.

Actionable Steps:

How to implement: Begin with the "why before what" ritual by keeping a small notebook at your workspace. Before starting any focused work session, spend exactly two minutes writing about why this specific task matters beyond immediate outcomes. Connect it to your values, not just your goals. Start with one work session daily for the first week, then expand to all major tasks.

When to do it: Implement this ritual at the beginning of your most important work block each day, ideally when your mental energy is highest. Set a phone reminder for this time. After one week of consistent practice, add the ritual before any task requiring more than 30 minutes of focused attention.

Why this works: Writing activates different neural pathways than thinking alone, creating stronger connections between tasks and values. The two-minute limit prevents overthinking while ensuring genuine reflection. Research shows that connecting work to personal meaning increases both performance quality and satisfaction by up to 33%.

How to implement: Create the "service connection" ritual by scheduling 15 minutes every Sunday to review your week's work and identify one specific way it could help someone else. Write down exactly who could benefit and how. Then take one small action—send an email sharing an insight, offer help to a colleague, or document a process that others could use.

When to do it: Sunday evenings work best, as they provide natural reflection time before the new week. Block this time in your calendar as a recurring appointment. If Sundays don't work, choose any consistent weekly time when you won't be rushed.

Why this works: Regular reflection on service transforms work from self-focused achievement to other-focused contribution. Taking immediate action, however small, creates a feedback loop that reinforces meaning. Studies show that people who regularly connect their work to helping others report 23% higher life satisfaction and 31% lower burnout rates.

How to implement: Establish the "presence pause" by setting a gentle reminder (like a soft chime on your phone) to sound every 90 minutes during your workday. When it sounds, stop for exactly 30 seconds. Take three deep breaths and mentally acknowledge the opportunity to engage fully with your next activity. No judgment, just recognition of the chance to bring complete attention to whatever follows.

When to do it: Start with three pause moments during your workday—mid-morning, after lunch, and mid-afternoon. After two weeks, you can add more or adjust timing based on your natural transition points. The key is consistency rather than frequency.

Why this works: Brief pauses reset your attention and prevent the gradual degradation of focus throughout the day. Acknowledging each activity as an opportunity shifts your brain from task-completion mode to engagement mode, improving both performance and satisfaction. The 30-second duration is long enough to create a mental shift but short enough to maintain momentum.

How to implement: Begin the "wisdom integration" ritual by choosing one principle from this chapter (such as Frankl's concept that we can always choose our response). Write it on an index card and place it where you'll see it daily. Each evening, spend five minutes journaling about how you applied or could have applied this principle during the day. At month's end, choose a new principle to explore.

When to do it: Select your monthly principle on the first day of each month. Do your five-minute evening reflection at the same time each night, ideally as part of your bedtime routine. This consistency makes the practice automatic rather than requiring daily decisions about when to reflect.

Why this works: Monthly focus on a single principle allows deep integration rather than surface-level understanding. Daily application transforms intellectual concepts into embodied wisdom. The evening timing leverages your brain's natural consolidation processes during sleep, strengthening the neural pathways associated with the principle you're practicing. Research indicates that focused practice on a single concept for 30 days creates lasting behavioral change in 67% of participants.

~TWENTY-TWO: Values-Driven Transformation~

I was reviewing quarterly earnings reports when the call came that would challenge everything I thought I knew about success. My colleague Sarah Chen's voice trembled as she recounted a conversation with her six-year-old daughter Emma. "She drew our family," Sarah said, "but made me tiny because I'm never home."

Sarah had achieved what most would consider extraordinary success. As a senior investment banker at a top Manhattan firm, she commanded respect and compensation that placed her in the top one percent of earners. Yet that simple drawing from her daughter exposed a painful truth: she had built her life around other people's definitions of success rather than her own values.

This disconnect between external achievement and internal alignment affects more people than we realize. Dr. Kelly Wilson's research at the University of Mississippi, published in the Journal of Contextual Behavioral Science (2010), reveals that "values-action discrepancy" doesn't just create unhappiness—it literally diminishes our capacity to experience positive emotions, even during objectively good moments. When our daily actions conflict with our core beliefs, our brains become less capable of experiencing satisfaction from any achievement.

Sarah's journey began at Wharton fifteen years earlier, where she absorbed the prevailing wisdom that success meant maximizing compensation and climbing corporate ladders. Her analytical brilliance and work ethic propelled her through the ranks, each promotion reinforcing the path she had chosen. But Dr. Tim Kasser's research, documented in "The High Price of Materialism" (MIT Press, 2002), shows that prioritizing extrinsic motivators like money and status over intrinsic ones like relationships and personal growth creates what he calls "materialistic value syndrome"—a pattern of psychological and physical deterioration.

The symptoms were all there in Sarah's life. Despite her corner office overlooking Central Park and compensation packages that exceeded most people's lifetime earnings, she felt increasingly empty. Her marriage showed strain as work demands consumed evenings and weekends. Even her health suffered, with stress-related insomnia and digestive issues becoming her constant companions. She found herself taking anxiety medication just to handle the pressure of deals that, deep down, she knew were enriching shareholders at the expense of workers and communities.

What made Sarah's situation particularly challenging was how golden handcuffs create psychological traps. Each bonus, each promotion, each accolade made it harder to question whether the path itself was wrong. The sunk cost fallacy—our tendency to continue behaviors based on past investments rather than future value—kept her locked in patterns that no longer served her. She had invested fifteen years building expertise in mergers and acquisitions, developing relationships with senior executives, and establishing a reputation as one of the best analysts in her field. Walking away felt like admitting those years were wasted.

I watched Sarah navigate her transformation over eighteen months, and her approach offers a masterclass in values-driven change. Rather than making an impulsive decision to quit, she began with what Dr. Herminia Ibarra calls "small experiments." Ibarra's research at London Business School, published in "Working Identity: Unconventional Strategies for Reinventing Your Career" (Harvard Business Review Press, 2003), shows that successful career changes happen through testing and learning, not through introspection alone.

Sarah started volunteering her financial expertise with a renewable energy startup on weekends. She joined the advisory board of a social impact fund focused on affordable housing. She began writing about sustainable investing on LinkedIn, testing whether these activities energized or drained her. Each experiment provided data about what truly mattered to her versus what she had been conditioned to value.

The renewable energy startup was particularly revealing. Founded by two MIT engineers who had developed breakthrough battery storage technology, they desperately needed someone who understood complex financial structures but shared their mission of accelerating clean energy adoption. Sarah found herself staying up late not because she had to, but because she was genuinely excited about modeling how their technology could make renewable energy cost-competitive with fossil fuels in developing markets.

The contrast was striking. When structuring deals that maximized short-term profits regardless of environmental impact, Sarah felt depleted even after successful closings. She would come home from closing a leveraged buyout that would result in thousands of layoffs and feel physically ill, despite the million-dollar bonus that followed. But when helping the renewable startup create financial models that balanced profit with purpose, she experienced energy and engagement she hadn't felt in years. Dr. Mauricio Delgado's neuroscience research at Rutgers University, published in Nature Neuroscience (2007), explains why: values-consistent decisions activate the ventromedial prefrontal cortex, creating lasting satisfaction that external rewards alone cannot match.

The advisory board position with the social impact fund provided another data point. This fund, started by a former Goldman Sachs partner who had experienced his own values crisis, focused on investments that generated both financial returns and measurable social benefit. Sarah discovered that she could apply the same rigorous analytical frameworks she had mastered in traditional finance to evaluate investments in affordable housing, education technology, and healthcare access. The intellectual challenge remained, but now it served purposes that aligned with her values.

Building tolerance for uncertainty proved crucial in Sarah's transition. Investment banking, despite its intensity, offered predictable rewards and clear advancement paths. Moving to a mission-driven startup meant accepting equity risk and undefined career trajectories. But research by Dr. Brené Brown, documented in "Daring Greatly" (Gotham Books, 2012), shows that "values clarity" creates courage that transcends fear. When we become crystal clear about what matters most, other people's confusion or disapproval becomes irrelevant noise rather than controlling factors.

Sarah developed a practice of writing in a values journal every Sunday, exploring questions like: "What would I regret not trying if I knew I couldn't fail?" and "What example do I want to set for Emma about following your convictions?" These reflections, based on techniques from Dr. Steven Hayes's Acceptance and Commitment Therapy research published in Behaviour Research and Therapy (2006), helped her distinguish between fear-based thinking and values-based thinking.

Sarah's financial preparation followed principles similar to those advocated by the Financial

Independence Retire Early (FIRE) movement. She and her husband had been saving aggressively, living on one income while banking the other, not knowing they were preparing for a values-driven career change. They had accumulated eighteen months of expenses in liquid savings and had paid off their mortgage early. This financial cushion meant she could accept a 40% salary reduction when the renewable energy startup offered her the CFO position, focusing on equity upside and mission alignment rather than immediate compensation.

The negotiation process itself reflected her values transformation. Instead of maximizing cash compensation as she had been trained to do, Sarah negotiated for flexible work arrangements that would allow her to attend Emma's school events, equity participation that aligned her interests with the company's long-term success, and a role in shaping the company's social impact strategy. The startup's founders, recognizing that her values alignment would translate into committed leadership, structured a package that prioritized shared success over short-term extraction.

The social pressure was intense. Peers questioned why anyone would voluntarily leave such a lucrative position. One managing director pulled her aside and said, "You're having a midlife crisis. Take a sabbatical if you need to, but don't throw away everything you've built." Family members worried about financial security and career trajectory. Her father, an immigrant who had sacrificed everything for financial stability, couldn't understand why she would "waste" her elite education on a risky startup.

But Sarah had developed what Dr. Amy Wrzesniewski at Yale calls "job crafting" skills—the ability to reshape how we think about and approach our work. Research published in the Academy of Management Review (2001) shows that people who actively craft their jobs to align with their values report higher satisfaction and performance. She began to see her financial expertise not as a tool for maximizing shareholder value at any cost, but as a capability that could accelerate positive change when applied to the right problems.

The results validated Sarah's courage. Within eighteen months, her renewable energy company secured major contracts with three Fortune 500 companies seeking to improve their environmental impact. The breakthrough came when Sarah structured an innovative financing model that allowed large corporations to install renewable energy systems with no upfront cost, paying for them through energy savings over time. This creative application of her financial expertise, now directed toward environmental benefit, opened markets that traditional approaches had failed to penetrate.

More importantly, the quality of her life transformed. Her daughter now proudly tells friends how "Mommy helps companies take better care of the planet." At a recent school career day, Emma introduced Sarah not as "an investment banker" but as "someone who fights climate change with math." Her marriage strengthened as work became energizing rather than depleting. The Sunday anxiety that had plagued her for years—that dread of returning to meaningful but soul-crushing work—disappeared entirely. Even her physical health improved as chronic stress gave way to purposeful engagement. She stopped needing anxiety medication and found that her insomnia resolved naturally when her daily activities aligned with her values.

I've observed similar patterns in other values-driven transformations. Jeff Weiner stepped down as LinkedIn's CEO to pursue what he called "compassionate management," teaching leadership to the next generation despite the prestige of his former role. His decision, chronicled in various Harvard Business Review articles (2018-2020), demonstrates that values-driven choices often require leaving comfortable positions that no longer serve our deeper purpose.

Howard Schultz's story at Starbucks, documented in "Pour Your Heart Into It" (Hyperion, 1997), provides another powerful example. Growing up in Brooklyn's housing projects, Schultz witnessed his father's dignity destroyed by jobs that offered no benefits or security. When he built Starbucks, he insisted on providing health insurance and stock options to part-time employees—a decision that seemed financially reckless but reflected his values around human dignity. That values-driven choice became a competitive advantage, creating employee loyalty and customer service that competitors couldn't match.

These transformations share critical elements identified by research. First, successful changers maintain their core competencies while redirecting them toward different purposes. Sarah didn't abandon her financial expertise; she applied it to environmental impact. Second, they build transition bridges through small experiments rather than sudden leaps. Third, they develop what psychologists call "identity flexibility"—seeing themselves as more than their current job titles.

Dr. Richard Bolles, author of "What Color Is Your Parachute?" (Ten Speed Press, updated annually since 1970), provides a framework for values inventory that I've seen work repeatedly. By analyzing peak experiences—moments when we feel most alive and engaged—we can identify patterns revealing our core values. Sarah discovered that her happiest professional moments involved using analytical skills to solve problems with broader social benefit, not just financial optimization.

The neuroscience of values-driven decisions reveals why alignment matters so profoundly. Dr. Matthew Lieberman's research at UCLA, published in

"Social: Why Our Brains Are Wired to Connect" (Crown, 2013), shows that when we repeatedly make choices conflicting with our values, the brain treats this as chronic stress. Cortisol levels remain elevated, sleep quality decreases, and we become more susceptible to anxiety and depression. Conversely, values-aligned choices create what researchers call "eudaimonic well-being"—the deep satisfaction that comes from living according to our truest beliefs.

Understanding these mechanisms helped me support others through similar transitions. The key insight is that values-driven transformation isn't about abandoning responsibility or pursuing naive idealism. It's about recognizing that sustainable success requires alignment between capabilities and convictions. When these align, work becomes energizing rather than draining, success feels meaningful rather than hollow, and we model authentic living for others.

The compound effect extends beyond individual satisfaction. People who make values-driven transitions often report discovering capacities they didn't know they possessed. Sarah found she could inspire teams through authentic passion in ways that spreadsheets and profit projections never could. Her technical skills didn't diminish; they became more powerful when applied to purposes that mattered to her. She developed new capabilities in public speaking, strategic communication, and cross-functional leadership that her narrow investment banking role had never required or developed.

Research by Dr. Shalom Schwartz, published in the Journal of Personality and Social Psychology (1992), identifies universal human values that transcend cultures and contexts. When we align our daily actions with these deeper values—whether focused on benevolence, universalism, achievement, or security—we tap into motivational reserves that external incentives cannot access. This explains why Sarah's productivity actually increased despite working in a more challenging, less structured environment.

The ripple effects of values-driven transformation extend beyond the individual making the change. Sarah's decision influenced several junior bankers who had been questioning their own career paths. Two of them eventually made their own transitions to impact investing and social enterprises. Her story became a case study at Wharton, challenging the next generation to think beyond traditional success metrics. Even her former colleagues, while initially skeptical, began incorporating environmental and social governance factors into their analyses, recognizing that these values-driven considerations were becoming essential to long-term business success.

The transformation from external validation to internal compass represents one of the most challenging yet rewarding journeys we can undertake. It requires courage to question success formulas that society reinforces through every promotion and bonus. It demands wisdom to distinguish between fear-based thinking ("What will people think?") and values-based thinking ("What kind of example do I want to set?"). Most crucially, it needs practical tools for navigating the transition without destroying the life we've built.

Values-driven transformation doesn't guarantee easier paths or immediate rewards. Sarah faced moments of doubt when startup challenges mounted and her former colleagues announced their latest bonuses. But she had discovered something more valuable than financial compensation: the energy that comes from alignment, the satisfaction of meaningful contribution, and the peace of living according to her deepest convictions. Her story reminds us that true success isn't about meeting others' expectations—it's about honoring our own values while creating positive impact in the world.

Actionable Steps:

How to implement: Begin with a values inventory by listing your ten most satisfying life experiences, then identify common themes. What values were being honored in these moments? Next, assess your current situation for values-action gaps by rating how well your daily activities align with identified values on a 1-10 scale. Design small experiments to test values alignment—volunteer your skills, take on different projects, or explore adjacent fields.

Track your energy levels during different activities, noting what energizes versus drains you. Create a values journal where you reflect weekly on decisions and their alignment with your core beliefs. Build financial runway by reducing expenses and increasing savings to create flexibility for potential transitions.

When to do it: Start the values inventory this weekend when you have two uninterrupted hours for reflection. Conduct values-action gap assessment within the next week. Begin one small experiment within two weeks, committing at least two hours weekly for two months. Schedule monthly review sessions to evaluate results and adjust experiments. Start the values journal immediately, spending 15 minutes each Sunday reflecting on the past week. Begin financial preparation now, regardless of transition timing, by automatically saving an additional 10% of income.

Why this works: Values clarity activates the brain's intrinsic motivation systems, creating sustainable energy for change. Small experiments reduce risk while providing real data about what energizes you. Regular energy tracking helps distinguish between temporary discomfort and fundamental misalignment. Monthly reviews prevent drift and ensure continuous progress toward authentic living. Values journaling strengthens neural pathways associated with purpose and meaning. Financial preparation reduces fear-based decision making, allowing values to guide choices. This systematic approach transforms vague dissatisfaction into actionable steps toward meaningful change while building the practical foundation necessary for successful transition.

~TWENTY-THREE: Finding Meaning Through Adversity~

The concept of finding meaning in suffering struck me as absurd when I first encountered it. How could anyone suggest that losing a loved one, battling illness, or facing financial ruin contained hidden gifts? The idea seemed like the worst kind of self-help platitude—until I discovered the scientific research that proves some people genuinely emerge from trauma not just recovered, but transformed.

The research comes from psychologists Richard Tedeschi and Lawrence Calhoun at the University of North Carolina, who coined the term "post-traumatic growth" in their groundbreaking 1995 study published in the Journal of Traumatic Stress. They discovered that significant numbers of trauma survivors report profound positive changes: deeper relationships, increased personal strength, greater appreciation for life, spiritual development, and new life possibilities. This wasn't wishful thinking—it was measurable psychological transformation documented across thousands of cases.

But understanding this intellectually and experiencing it personally are vastly different things. The bridge between knowledge and transformation became clear to me through studying Viktor Frankl's experiences, detailed in his 1946 book "Man's Search for Meaning" (originally published in German as "Ein Psycholog erlebt das

Konzentrationslager"). Frankl, an Austrian psychiatrist, survived multiple Nazi concentration camps including Auschwitz and Dachau. While imprisoned, he observed that survival wasn't determined by physical strength or even luck—it correlated most strongly with the ability to find meaning in the experience.

Frankl noticed that prisoners who maintained some sense of purpose—whether reuniting with family, completing unfinished work, or bearing witness to atrocities—survived at higher rates than those who lost all sense of meaning. He developed his theory of logotherapy based on these observations, arguing that humans' primary drive isn't pleasure (as Freud suggested) or power (as Adler claimed), but the search for meaning.

"Everything can be taken from a man but one thing," Frankl wrote, "the last of human freedoms—to choose one's attitude in any given set of circumstances, to choose one's own way." This wasn't abstract philosophy developed in comfortable academic settings. This was wisdom forged in humanity's darkest hour, tested against the most extreme suffering imaginable.

The neuroscience supporting Frankl's observations emerged decades later. A 2014 study by Dr. Martin Seligman and colleagues at the University of Pennsylvania, published in the Journal of Positive Psychology, used fMRI scanning to observe brain activity during meaning-making exercises. They found that when people actively searched for meaning in difficult experiences, specific neural networks activated—particularly in the prefrontal cortex and anterior cingulate cortex, regions associated with executive function and emotional regulation.

These "meaning-making networks" literally rewire our brains' response to trauma. Instead of becoming stuck in fear-based neural loops, the brain develops new pathways that integrate difficult experiences into a coherent life narrative. This isn't about denying pain or pretending suffering is good—it's about the brain's capacity to extract learning and growth from any experience.

Consider Malala Yousafzai's transformation after being shot by the Taliban in 2012 for advocating girls' education in Pakistan. Her story, documented in her 2013 autobiography "I Am Malala" (co-written with Christina Lamb), demonstrates how devastating trauma can catalyze profound purpose. Rather than being silenced by violence, she became a global advocate for education, winning the Nobel Peace Prize at age seventeen.

Yousafzai didn't minimize her trauma or claim everything happened for a reason. She acknowledged the terror, pain, and long recovery. But she made a conscious choice to transform her suffering into fuel for her mission. "They thought that the bullets would silence us," she said in her

2013 United Nations speech. "But they failed. And out of that silence came thousands of voices."

This transformation process follows predictable patterns that researchers have documented across cultures and types of trauma. Dr. Stephen Joseph's 2011 book "What Doesn't Kill Us: The New Psychology of Posttraumatic Growth" synthesizes decades of research showing that growth typically occurs in specific stages. First comes the shattering of assumptions—trauma breaks our beliefs about how the world works. Then comes the struggle to make sense of what happened. Finally, if conditions are right, comes the rebuilding of worldview that incorporates the trauma into a meaningful narrative.

The conditions that support this transformation are crucial. Joseph's research, along with a 2010 meta-analysis by Prati and Pietrantoni published in Clinical Psychology Review, identifies key factors: social support, the ability to express emotions, active coping strategies, and what they call "deliberate rumination"—purposeful reflection on the experience rather than intrusive, repetitive thoughts.

Sheryl Sandberg's journey after losing her husband suddenly in 2015 illustrates these principles in action. Her book "Option B" (2017, co-authored with psychologist Adam Grant) documents her path from devastating grief to what she calls "post-traumatic growth." Sandberg didn't just survive her loss—she developed deeper empathy, stronger connections with her children, and a mission to help others navigate adversity.

What made Sandberg's transformation possible wasn't positive thinking or time alone. She actively engaged in meaning-making practices: journaling about her emotions, seeking therapy, connecting with others who had experienced loss, and eventually channeling her experience into helping others. She writes about learning to "kick the shit out of Option B"—not because Option B is ideal, but because it's the reality we must work with.

The research on journaling's role in post-traumatic growth is particularly compelling. Dr. James Pennebaker's studies at the University of Texas, published in journals including the Journal of Personality and Social Psychology (1997), show that expressive writing about trauma improves both physical and mental health. The act of constructing a coherent narrative from chaotic experience literally changes how our brains process the trauma.

But meaning-making isn't just an individual process. The social dimension proves equally crucial. Dr. Lawrence Calhoun's 2013 research published in Psychological Inquiry found that trauma survivors who share their stories in supportive environments show significantly higher rates of post-traumatic growth. The act of witnessing and being witnessed transforms personal pain into shared wisdom.

This principle explains why support groups prove so effective for everything from addiction recovery to grief processing. When we hear others articulate experiences similar to ours, we realize we're not uniquely broken. When we share our own stories and see them help others, our suffering gains purpose beyond ourselves.

The story of Cheryl Strayed, chronicled in her 2012 memoir "Wild: From Lost to Found on the Pacific Crest Trail," powerfully illustrates this transformation. After her mother died from cancer and her life spiraled into heroin use and destructive behavior, Strayed hiked 1,100 miles of the Pacific Crest Trail alone. The physical journey became a crucible for processing grief and reclaiming her life.

Strayed didn't find easy answers on the trail. She writes about blisters, exhaustion, fear, and the constant temptation to quit. But through facing these external challenges, she developed the strength to face her internal ones. The trail forced her to sit with her grief rather than escape it through drugs or destructive relationships. By the journey's end, she hadn't "gotten over" her mother's death—she had learned to carry it differently.

"How wild it was, to let it be," Strayed writes, capturing the paradox of acceptance. Letting difficult experiences "be" doesn't mean passive resignation. It means acknowledging reality fully enough to work with it rather than against it. This acceptance creates the foundation for transformation.

Dr. Edith Eger's story, detailed in her 2017 book "The Choice: Embrace the Possible," provides perhaps the most extreme example of finding meaning through adversity. An Auschwitz survivor who became a psychologist, Eger was forced to dance for Josef Mengele the same night her parents were sent to the gas chambers. Decades later, she returned to Auschwitz not as a victim but as a healer, helping others process their own traumas.

Eger distinguishes between victimization (what happened to us) and victimhood (how we relate to what happened). "We cannot choose to have a life free of hurt," she writes. "But we can choose to be free, to escape the past, no matter what befalls us, and to embrace the possible."

This distinction proves crucial for understanding post-traumatic growth. We don't choose our traumas, but we can choose how we metabolize them. Eger developed what she calls "choice therapy," helping clients recognize that even in the worst circumstances, we retain the power to choose our response. This isn't about blame or suggesting people choose their suffering—it's about reclaiming agency in how we engage with unavoidable pain.

The biological mechanisms underlying post-traumatic growth continue to emerge through research. A 2016 study by Zannas and colleagues published in Nature Neuroscience found that trauma can trigger epigenetic changes—modifications in how genes are expressed. While some changes increase vulnerability to mental illness, others appear to enhance resilience and adaptive capacity. Our responses to trauma literally reshape our biology, for better or worse.

This research suggests that how we engage with adversity matters at the cellular level. Chronic victimhood and rumination activate inflammatory pathways linked to depression and illness. But meaning-making and growth-oriented coping activate different biological systems associated with health and vitality. We're not just changing our minds when we transform trauma into meaning—we're changing our bodies.

The practical implications are profound. Instead of viewing trauma as purely damaging, we can approach it as potential catalyst for growth—while still acknowledging its genuine difficulty and pain. This doesn't mean seeking out suffering or minimizing others' pain. It means developing tools to transform unavoidable suffering into wisdom and strength.

Nelson Mandela's transformation during 27 years of imprisonment exemplifies this principle on a grand scale. His autobiography "Long Walk to Freedom" (1994) documents how he used his incarceration to develop the patience, wisdom, and moral authority that would later enable him to lead South Africa's peaceful transition from apartheid. He emerged not bitter but refined, using his suffering to develop qualities that served millions.

"There is nothing like returning to a place that remains unchanged to find the ways in which you yourself have altered," Mandela wrote. The prison didn't change—he did. Through decades of confinement, he transformed from an angry young revolutionary into a statesman capable of leading reconciliation between oppressor and oppressed.

The research consistently shows that post-traumatic growth isn't rare or reserved for exceptional people. A 2004 meta-analysis by Linley and Joseph in Psychological Assessment found that 30-70% of trauma survivors report at least some positive change. The variance depends on trauma type, available support, and individual factors, but the capacity for growth appears universal.

Understanding these patterns changed how I approach my own challenges. Instead of asking "Why is this happening to me?" I learned to ask "What might this be teaching me?" Instead of rushing to feel better, I practiced sitting with difficulty long enough to extract its lessons. Instead of hiding my struggles, I began sharing them in ways that might help others.

This shift requires what researchers call "constructive rumination"—actively working to make sense of experiences rather than passively replaying them. It's the difference between being stuck in a mental loop and actively mining experience for wisdom. The former deepens trauma; the latter transforms it.

The transformation doesn't happen overnight. Tedeschi and Calhoun's research shows that post-traumatic growth typically unfolds over months or years, not days or weeks. It requires patience with ourselves as we slowly reconstruct meaning from shattered assumptions. It demands gentleness as we learn to hold both pain and growth simultaneously.

Most importantly, finding meaning through adversity isn't about reaching a destination where pain disappears. It's about developing the capacity to transform suffering into significance, to metabolize poison into medicine, to alchemize lead into gold. The pain remains real, but it no longer defines us. Instead, it becomes part of a larger story of resilience, growth, and service to others walking similar paths.

Actionable Steps:

How to implement: Begin a structured meaning-making practice through daily journaling. Write for 15-20 minutes about a current or past challenge, focusing on three prompts: "What is this experience teaching me about my values and strengths?" "How might this difficulty be preparing me to help others?" "What would it look like to embrace this reality while still working toward positive change?"

Write continuously without editing or censoring. After one week, review your entries for patterns and insights.

When to do it: Start this practice immediately upon recognizing you're facing a significant challenge, or retrospectively for past traumas you haven't fully processed. Perform the writing at the same time each day, ideally when you won't be interrupted. Continue for at least 30 days to allow patterns and insights to emerge. Many find evening most effective for reflection, but choose whatever time you can protect consistently.

Why this works: Research by Pennebaker and others demonstrates that expressive writing helps organize chaotic experiences into coherent narratives, reducing intrusive thoughts and improving both mental and physical health. The specific prompts guide constructive rumination rather than passive replay. Daily practice builds neural pathways for meaning-making, literally rewiring your brain's response to adversity. The 30-day timeline allows sufficient repetition for new patterns to stabilize while being short enough to maintain commitment.

www.ingramcontent.com/pod-product-compliance
Lightning Source LLC
Chambersburg PA
CBHW050855160426
43194CB00011B/2163